The Penelope Theory of Architecture

—

SCI-Arc has never considered itself a school built on consensus, no matter how egalitarian or fashionable that concept appears to be. We are not a school which attempts to achieve harmony by neatly balancing a number of opposing opinions. In fact, harmony here is irrelevant. We make choices. We have preferences in the culture and in the city. We are prepared to be advocates, to take positions, both in the academy and on the street.

We stand here today, on the east edge of downtown Los Angeles, and can turn our heads to face County Jail, USC Hospital, LA's concrete river, the Amtrak site, Boyle Heights, the Alameda Corridor, USC, the Geffen, MOCA, Bunker Hill, and so on. We are situated at an urban pivot point, a confluence of races, politics and urban tactics. And our presence here confirms the courage of the SCI-Arc advocacy.

A group of board members, faculty and students took SCI-Arc from the affluent Westside of Los Angeles to the densest of cultural intersections in a heretofore forbidden and foreboding part of the city. Downtown SCI-Arc is a voice for the alternative city, for a reinvented conception of the city's purpose. And, make no mistake, this is not a theoretical position.

▶

We will live by our decision, fiscally and sociologically, or we will cease to exist.

Count on our continued existence.

SCI-Arc is its advocacy. That's the first, and perhaps primary lesson here, in defiance of the historic admonition that insists on the separation of "the street" and "the academy." SCI-Arc put the academy in the street.

The world as SCI-Arc interprets it — art, politics, economics, and sociology — is not only what we are told the world is, but what we tell the world it needs to be. And the world we choose to make is also for people who aren't born yet. Don't forget that. SCI-Arc's new downtown home says all of that unequivocally.

To repeat a few words from an introduction once given to the work of Office dA, because I think they represent an epiphany of the important message the SCI-Arc community continues to deliver:

> Architecture moves.
>
> That doesn't mean up or down.
> That doesn't mean forward or back.
> That doesn't mean left or right or better or worse.
>
> But the contents, the emphasis, the form language, and the means of representation continue to evolve.
>
> How does that happen?
> Who says what architecture is?

And my answer to you is this: We say.

SCI-Arc will always play a substantive role in the discourse and definition of contemporary architecture: Collectively as an institution; individually in the professional achievements of its faculty and in the acts of imagination and invention of its students.

We joined that debate in 1972. We will continue to reformulate it thirty years later.

SCI-Arc makes architecture dance.

How has that happened in the past? How will that process continue in the future?

There are those who believe that SCI-Arc's history is the history of a number of remarkable individuals whose unique professional efforts describe the institution's point of view. SCI-Arc has such individuals. SCI-Arc was founded on the achievements of such individuals. SCI-Arc continues to discover such individuals. In fact, I am confident that the SCI-Arc environment is a primary collector and progenitor of both character and characters. We will continue to pursue both.

There are others who argue that academic success originates in a carefully prescribed pedagogy — formulae, obligations, rules, and tools that provide the intellectual and organizational guidelines that point us toward our objectives. We are building that pedagogy with our board, faculty, and students.

But please keep in mind that the construction of pedagogy is perpetual and the destination ever elusive. Recall Penelope,

▶

Odysseus' wife: While Odysseus was gone for twenty years, Penelope was pursued by various less than appealing suitors. She promised to marry one when she completed the knitting of a tapestry, which she carefully wove during the day and carefully took apart at night.

That's the SCI-Arc metaphor.

We pull together; we coalesce; we pull apart — and this metaphysical assembly/disassembly manifests itself daily in lectures, exhibits, building, publishing, teaching and debate.

SCI-Arc is the Penelope Theory of architecture.

Consider Christopher Columbus on his first trip (looking for India/encountering America), or Columbus on his second trip (a journey to a destination that could now be anticipated at the outset). Columbus on his first trip is the SCI-Arc metaphor: A discovery process which begins to formulate a paradigm but is simultaneously open and amenable to a different, newly emerging, and perhaps entirely contradictory prospect.

For SCI-Arc, surprise is no surprise.

SCI-Arc stands for a perpetual dismantling of architectural allegiances.

SCI-Arc has no permanent friends or enemies in poetry, time, or space.

SCI-Arc is constantly re-pointed at a transitory target: Building, buildings, and building cities.

▶

SCI-Arc will be a creative voice for evolving paradigms of culture and building, using Los Angeles as an experimental field with a constantly renewed community of faculty and students who continue to make it new.

Who says what architecture is?

———————

SCI-Arc Graduation speech, May 19, 2002

WHO SAYS WHAT ARCHITECTURE IS?

Eric Owen Moss

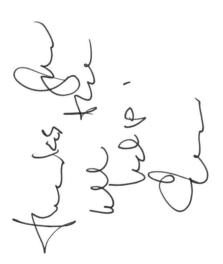

Edited by Julianna Morais
SCI-Arc Press
Los Angeles, California

Published by the SCI-Arc Press
Southern California Institute of Architecture
960 East 3rd Street
Los Angeles, California 90013
www.sciarc.edu

ISBN 0-9760079-4-0

Editor: Julianna Morais
Typography: Brian Roettinger
Cover Design: Eric Owen Moss
Copy Editor: Martha Read

—

Library of Congress Cataloging-in-Publication Data

Moss, Eric Owen, 1943–
  Who says what architecture is? / Eric Owen Moss ; edited by
 Julianna Morais. – 1st pbk. ed.
    p. cm.
ISBN 0-9760079-4-0 (pbk. : alk. paper)
1. Architecture. I. Morais, Julianna. II. Title.

NA2560.M62 2007
720–dc22
                         2007033166

Emily
Miller
Addison

In Sight of the Invisible [mhm]

Contents

You Can't Pick Your Birthday

Michael Maltzan

—

We are now midway into the Los Angeles Architecture Revolution.

So what's the role of the midway man in a revolution?

What's experiment?

How about:
Overrule the rule;
Or impulse over method;
Or instinct over system.

Before experiments are entitled, they're unratified musings, speculations. If the speculations survive, on to sketches and models. Surviving that, small buildings begin to designate an alternative form language.

As that tentative vocabulary is defined and built, the vocabulary itself becomes a subject that is taught and learned...

... and as a learned vocabulary, it becomes:
less impulse, more method;
less instinct, more system;
less overrule the rule, more ruled;
and in the end, a doctrine.

So the revolution either disappears before it begins, or, inevitably, becomes doctrine. And in the interim, it draws adherents who come to practice the impulse, but remain to practice the method.

In neither case can the revolution run interminably. Or can it?

You can't pick your birthday.

The inadvertent midway man offers us a historic option: Don't memo-rize the lesson. Amend it.

Viva la revolution.

Because you can't pick your birthday.

Introduction to Michael Maltzan lecture, SCI-Arc, September 27, 2006.

The Architecture Free Zone
—

Los Angeles — The sprawl quotient: Take off from JFK heading west and you're immediately over Los Angeles.

Los Angeles — The homogeneity quotient: Drive the LA freeways; get off at the right exit, get off at the wrong exit, it doesn't make any difference.

Los Angeles is a city for architects. But Los Angeles is not necessarily a city for architecture.

The Culver City/Los Angeles project area is an immense hodgepodge of industrial and manufacturing buildings, constructed in the 1930s and '40s, outlined by railroad tracks, the river, long boulevards, and the power grid. The mostly abandoned warehouses are themselves a category of infrastructure here. The site was originally served by Southern Pacific Railway freight trains running east and west on the median strip of National Boulevard.

Los Angeles is an infant city.

That means its priorities, its hierarchies, its sense of focus are not fixed, but variable. Comparisons to other cities around the world miss that point. Note the relatively swift rise in attention to the most disparate areas in the city (and often, a concomitant attention shift away): Westwood, Warner Center, the Sunset Strip, Melrose Avenue, Century City, and today, downtown Los Angeles. Priorities and interest are on the move, as is urban investment and the political attention span.

In a context of fluid urban emphases, Culver City/Los Angeles became immediately plausible: The latest hot spot. Culver City, once
a manufacturing and industrial *somewhere* became an abandoned
ex-industrial *nowhere,* and again a burgeoning urban *somewhere*:
An instantly viable option for experimental art and commerce on
the Westside of Los Angeles. In cities with a more recognizable *pro
forma* — with durable downtowns, midtowns, loops, 5th Avenues,
Ringstraßes, Champs-Elysées, Ramblas, and so on — the prospect of
beginning a substantial new alternative, competitive with an established model, is less plausible. But in Los Angeles, that change of em-
phasis provides new opportunity in a new venue for aspiring young
businesses and artistic talents, along with more established versions
of the same who are prepared to participate in the perpetual reform-
ing of the city's character.

The East Culver City/Central Los Angeles project site existed in a
deserted state in the early 1990s. Manufacturing and industry in
Los Angeles, and in the US and Europe, dissipated and finally disappeared, leaving that deteriorating mass of warehouses, railway
rights of way, empty streets, and a graffiti-covered, concrete river
bed.

Culver City/LA is an economic prototype, repeating conditions
typical in contemporary Western cities from ex-East Berlin to the
dockyards of London; Brooklyn, Bedford Stuyvesant, and the South
Bronx in NY; to the south side of Chicago; east side of St. Louis; San
Francisco south of Market, and so on. These are all areas where industry and manufacturing have vacated in favor of cheap labor and
minimum controls on the environment and working conditions in
Mexico, Korea, China, and India.

The NAFTA Canada/US/Mexico trade and commerce prototype in
effect precipitates the abandoning of America's industrial zones.
How to resuscitate, rehabilitate, reconstitute, revitalize, and recon-
ceive those zones?

*The perpetual variability of the master plan represents the continuing
variability of production, distribution, and consumption around the*

world. In effect, no master plan.

In 1989, when the current Moss project began, we designated the project an "Architecture Free Zone."

Initially, there was little sense that an effort of substantial city re-conception was in the offing. We simply began to work on several simple additions and subtractions to that existing body of contiguous warehouses. Only in retrospect was the project didactic.

The strategic aspiration of the Architecture Free Zone was that no *a priori* planning or building regulations from either Los Angeles or Culver City would apply *ipso facto* to the project. Rather, each planned component would be based on a particular conceptual strategy for that portion of the project, and would be presented and debated with city officials, developers, and other consultants.

The case for each project was the case for each project. No urban precedents. No urban antecedents. No history lessons. The fact that a particular case was substantiated and accepted never guaranteed that precedent would warranty "another one of those." Each planning argument modified arguments that preceded it as the context evolved. There were no relationship requirements, height requirements, area requirements, use requirements, setbacks or parking criteria. Any and all of those, to the extent they were relevant, would all be subject to the evolving conceptual discourse. As the area grew, it became the associations, the interconnections between the components, rather than any single building strategy, that determined the developing development rules.

The project is a race with a moving finish line. The *pro forma* at any point was provisional, deterministic only with respect to an ongoing project, but of limited durability.

We call the plan the Provisional Paradigm.

As we studied the site, we began to think in terms of reconceiving the surrounding infrastructure. The railway route, boulevards, power grid, and river components could no longer operate satisfactorily simply as civil engineering solutions to the technical problems of water movement, providing electricity, and moving cars and trains. Technical purposes had never been evaluated beyond their utilitarian aspect. Infrastructure's capacity to divide and segregate the city had to be ameliorated. We decided to build on the railway spur and in and over the concrete river.

The operational principle for Culver City/LA was that the infrastructure should become the foundation for new building types, strategically reconnecting areas that the engineers divided. The Southern Pacific Air Rights City, the LA River crossing project between Los Angeles and Culver City, and the 110 meter long air rights structure for Cineon Kodak are supra-infrastructure initiatives.

The project was never architecture *qua* architecture, but always architecture as a means to identify the new social and civic opportunities in the area. Production facilities house associated companies in media, advertising, film, communication, music, and the performing arts, who share stages, changeable office space, eating facilities, and outdoor event venues.

We continue to conceive relationships between roads, tracks, rivers, and warehouse buildings — dividing, demolishing, building over, under, around and through — so that the nexus of structures conveys in perpetuity the concept of reinventing — reconnected, rescaled, redefined.

All this is logistically possible because the owners control vast contiguous areas and have purchased the intermittent properties, so none of the conventional zoning — property by property — designations have ever been applicable to the conception of the project.

The scale of building has recently increased as high density concepts have replaced the need to reuse the original warehouse stock. Freight train routes through the area will reappear as on-grade passenger lines. Two connected high-rises on the Los Angeles side of the concrete river will soon join a lived-in LA/Culver City Bridge. And a three theater concert hall adjoining a new, half-mile long ex-railway right-of-way park with an outdoor amphitheater are on the way.

The paradigm remains provisional. The Architecture Free Zone is intact. And no master plan has yet appeared.

Originally written for the LA/Culver City exhibit featured at the 2006 Venice Biennale.

Pump Up the River

—

Los Angeles is a city of innovative architecture, but it is defined less by buildings than by the enormous scale of its infrastructure — railways, waterworks, power grids and, of course, the ubiquitous freeways.

It all addresses obvious practical problems: How to move cars, water, power and trains. But the unintended consequence is *de facto* "zoning by infrastructure" — subdivisions of use, sociology, affluence and poverty, unanticipated by the engineers who planned the concrete rivers and freeways.

Let's reimagine the infrastructure. Let's conceive of it no longer simply as a way to solve technical problems but as a multipurpose planning-and-design instrument to reconnect disparate zones of the city.

Where to begin?

The LA River, that Maginot Line of poured concrete and infrequent high water that winds from the mountains to the ocean.

Make the river a public amenity. Dam it. Sail in it. Bring adjacent communities to its edges. Bridge it, and inhabit the bridges — commerce, recreation, housing and education will span the renewed river. Clean the water, store it, and then release it as a source of hydroelectric power.

Where to start?

Between the 1st Street and 6th Street bridges, where the river separates Latino Boyle Heights and downtown. Join the communities at the river.

Opinion piece, *Los Angeles Times*, December 27, 2006.

Surreal LA

Richard Meier

—

In transit through west LA, driving north on the 405: To the east, one or two nondescript curtain walls; to the west, at Sunset, a Holiday Inn fills the local cylinder quotient; and strung across the hills, numberless single family homes offer us the "more of the same" developer *pro forma*.

But wait a minute... The focus of this otherwise routine Los Angeles vista is an astonishing anomaly that appears to abscond with the local hilltops.

Is the Getty surreal?

I notice, surely we have all noticed, an ever increasing dependence on the now ubiquitous "surreal," a designation originally authored by André Breton. That once succinct aesthetic category has become an uncritical vaguery and perhaps, ultimately, a banality.

So surrealism, once an attempt to label the fragile conceptual unity of private introspection and public artistic expression, has more recently become a commentator's slogan for anything that slightly varies from the ordinary, however superficially. And, by the way, the label is now considered an unadulterated compliment.

I would like to request some critical artistic censorship: I'm calling for a Los Angeles reassessment of the term "surreal," banning that adjective except at rare and exclusive moments when what is produced is, in Breton's terms, "marvelous," and where the "marvelous becomes beautiful," and, more important, "dangerous."

And where do we locate that art today?

The original surreal is surreal no longer. *To relocate it, we have to discontinue our search in the collected reruns of Magritte, Man Ray, Max Ernst, de Chirico and others and to look where we haven't been taught to look — along the 405, for instance.*

Breton characterized the surrealist's relationship to history: That interrelationship between time and eternity, he said, consists of a series of subjective and objective assaults, and creates that rare and marvelous world which belongs to history and supersedes it; sustains and rejects; accepts and reimagines; and in so doing, sometimes (but rarely) becomes its own idiosyncratic chapter that removes and moves the definition of architecture.

Introduction to Richard Meier lecture, LACMA (Los Angeles County Museum of Art), April 29, 2005.

The SCI-Arc Situation / The LA Situation
—

SCI-Arc is located on Santa Fe Avenue in downtown Los Angeles, in a building that runs about a quarter mile in length. There is a vacant, eight-acre piece of property to the west, where staff, faculty and students have rested their automobiles, undisturbed, for three years. Confronted with a "No Trespassing" sign that recently appeared on the adjacent property, I speculated with several members of the Board of Directors of SCI-Arc about what steps might be required, faced with an adversarial neighbor.

The SCI-Arc situation is symptomatic of a more general tension in the city's planning process. *So I'd like to tie the uncertain future of SCI-Arc downtown to the discussion of the city's future in the broadest sense — what the city might become, and why, and how we might get there.* Inevitably, I'll have to generalize and draw conclusions to which there are obvious exceptions. This is a city of subtlety, nuance, and contradiction. Nevertheless, I think the first operational principle is: "We've only just begun." The future is in front of us.

I don't know that LA would ever be characterized as a bastion of physical beauty. But there is a poetic quality, from a certain distance on a certain day at a certain time, an ethereal sense of what the city is: Not distilled or fixed, and it hasn't been assigned a particular consequence. It's fluid. To borrow the much used metaphor, it's an extraordinary horizontal canvas, and I think there is a unique opportunity in front of us today to reimagine that canvas.

There has been a lot of discussion, accompanied by the occasionally facetious cartoon or caricature, of Los Angeles as a city in motion. The city constructs, and, before the concrete settles, it reconstructs, and so on. The ability to keep the city conceptually moving suggests a collective apprehension for what is durable, and is a useful element in the perpetual rethinking of the city. Maybe we are coming to the point and the time when our generation will say evolving conceptions of downtown have ended. Movement's over. It's a fixed priority. But for the moment, that fluidity, that long-term indecisiveness, is one of the ingredients that makes this city what it is.

And there isn't any dependable *pro forma* that guides the relationship between the existing city and its additions (or subtractions), either in style, content, or scale. That's an intellectual asset. It makes change a debate, not a rule system.

And something else that's essential for a city in process to understand: The difference between the current city and the next city is not substantial in time. *Old is not much older than new. Or new is not much newer than old.* LA is not a "historic" city, notwithstanding a number of people who would like to evaluate the state of LA's evolution with respect to cities which belong to traditions that run back hundreds of years. That sort of evaluative perspective takes us in the wrong conceptual direction. We want to understand what we are and what we're capable of, measured against our own moving perspective, not against someone else's travel brochure. There's no externally derived *pro forma* for Los Angeles. We should imagine our own.

And then there's the LA suburban discussion that you all know, that you've heard over and over: Endless interchangeable horizontality, single family houses *über alles*, the ubiquitous automobile, suggesting a time when Los Angeles understood itself largely as a collection of suburbs. "LA: The Suburb" was never the whole story. But if in former times there was some accuracy in the suburban prognosis, that's no longer the case. Something else is on the move.

The census statement indicates the city is growing rapidly. So we ought to keep in mind that the city we study, the city we attempt to understand, is not a fixed condition. The population is moving. So the solution(s) have to acknowledge not only where we are, but what might be coming next.

Los Angeles is a fertile field for urban prognosis, urban intellectualizing, and urban philosophizing. LA is often someone's city of the future. Analytical models of Los Angeles projected on Los Angeles from outside Los Angeles frequently arrive from very different urban *pro forma*s. As if one could say, "If Los Angeles had this" and "If Los Angeles had that," it then fit the foreign analog model. Absent those organizational "fits," Los Angeles is not there yet. This exemplifies a continuous effort to define the city by applying priorities that originate elsewhere. That sort of analysis is likely to miss what is original here, by insisting on determining LA's progress based on its capacity to subsume an external model.

LA on the couch imagines Los Angeles as a psychiatric patient. If it were possible to assign the city a single persona, and if it were possible to put that persona on the couch, then conceivably, LA is a persona in conflict. *Should the city subscribe to an external model of what the city should be, or should the city apply its demonstrable inventive capacity in conjunction with the idiosyncrasies of this urban circumstance to imagine the city uniquely, and broadcast that conceptual message, as opposed to retrieving what originated elsewhere and attempting to implement that?*

A generic perspective presumes there are essential organizational components that consistently belong to the discourse on big cities. Let's call them urban assets and liabilities. If you share the assets and correct the liabilities, you are recognized as urbanistically legitimate. LA has never quite accommodated the generic model, nor has it decided whether to aspire to that model or to make its own way. The effort to define LA as a part of a club or a group, or as a way of reinterpreting world cities, inevitably comes up a downtown or a transit system short. The real strength here is in the prospect of idiosyncrasy this city has to offer its own future, and as an alternative model to the world.

We're not NYC, nor do we have a Fifth Avenue, although there was a time, in the late 1940s, when planners thought that the Wilshire Boulevard Miracle Mile might become our Fifth Avenue. Nor are we Paris and the Champs-Elysées. Nor are we Las Ramblas in Barcelona or the Ringstraße in Vienna. The instinct to measure Los Angeles against cities which are as different from each other as they are from LA weakens the Los Angeles case and results in an urban inferiority complex.

Adulation of the external model is what LA should avoid.

There's another side to this introvert/extrovert discussion, an important one, which runs over the last ten to fifteen years. It has to do with the design conviction and imagination on exhibit in Los Angeles — which begins to suggest the making of a city plan an urban strategy — and individual pieces of architecture we're now sending around the world. There's Michele Saee in Paris, Thom Mayne in Madrid, Frank Gehry in Berlin, Craig Hodgetts and Ming Fung in Tokyo, and Eric Moss in Mexico City. Los Angeles ought to define itself today as a laboratory for urban experimentation. And this sense of inquiry extends beyond architecture and planning to the environmental audaciousness of Los Angeles as a site for a city. *LA is an invention in the desert.* We're at the early stages of that investigatory process, however the Sierra Club may object, in retrospect.

A word about *structure/infrastructure*. Structure here refers to the political organization of the city, how public policy decisions are made here. Infrastructure refers to the freeways, railway rights-of-way, the LA River, utilities and utility rights-of-way. There are five supervisorial and fifteen city council districts. LA County Supervisorial authority and LA City Council authority overlay one another and often confuse and contradict responsibilities. Interspersed with county and city jurisdictions are a number of independent civic jurisdictions: Glendale, Burbank, West Hollywood, Culver City, Beverly Hills, and Santa Monica. So clearly, the capacity to make large-scale transportation or utility or building/planning decisions is obviated by this *mélange* of intersecting and overlapping political jurisdictions, each with its own priorities, budgets, and constituents. That happenstance structure often results in piecemeal decision-making, which continues to deliver urban policy in fragments.

We should practice exploiting the fragments.

And there's the natural and man-made geography that defines LA. The Pacific Ocean is the edge of the city. Although it defines the area environmentally, access is limited. The Santa Monica Mountains separate the San Fernando Valley from the central city. The LA River, once free flowing, and from time to time overflowing, is now encased in a massive concrete structure that runs from the east edge of the city to the Santa Monica Bay. In addition, there are the ubiquitous power grids — endless poles and wires — the railway rights-of-ways, and the tracks, and the freeways.

If the political structure pulls the city apart, the infrastructure — the power grid, the river, the tracks, and the freeways — is a potential synthesizer. Traditional infrastructure problems and solutions are always defined in simple, civil engineering terms: Number of freeway lanes, freeway access, kilowatt-hours, prospect of river overflow, and so on. The engineered solutions to technical issues produce infrastructure that dominates the city but has little to do with any livability quotient. Meaning, *Los Angeles is organized at the urban scale by mammoth technical solutions to civil engineering questions.* The next step must be to redefine the infrastructure — the concrete riverbeds, the freeway and railway rights-of-way — as foundations that support the next generation of housing, recreation, commercial, and cultural construction in the city.

Another fundamental infrastructure component is the city's boulevards: Western, Sepulveda, La Cienega — north/south; Ventura, Sunset, Wilshire, and Olympic — east/west. The boulevards associate the widest range of urban sociologies along their routes, in contrast to the freeways, which run over or under the local sociologies.

I'd like to talk about a hypothesis that returns us to the city as youthful, or "fresh," in the current lexicon. There are periodic bursts of energy and construction in various, sometimes unanticipated parts of the city which, over a brief period of years, dissipate and dissolve, to be replaced by new bursts of energy and development in other areas — again, unsustained. Melrose Avenue, once the hippest of the hip, has dissipated as the hipness quotient has moved on, as hipness tends to do. The Sunset Strip has metamorphosed on a number of sometimes contradictory occasions — as a movietown club scene, as a rock and disco hotspot, and recently as affluent society housing, restaurants, and hotels. The Ambassador Hotel — which for some holds a poignant Kennedy family pedigree in addition to its association with Miracle Mile — has been entirely demolished, as has the original Miracle Mile Fifth Avenue hypothesis. The on-again/off-again remaking of these areas offers a perpetual sense of urban re-renewal. Durability of conception is limited here.

But I can't promise durability of renewal either. I think the change-ability quotient, *LA Hot and Cold*, has been the *pro forma* for years. We'll see at what point in time the variability coagulates, and reaffirms its priorities. I would like to suggest two venues where that might take place: On Grand Avenue and at SCI-Arc. What's important in both of these projects is the unique opportunity to sustain both the LA experiment and a durable urban result.

SCI-Arc occupies one of the most promising venues in the city for planning and design intervention, with the railway right-of-way to the east, and beyond that, the concrete LA River, and the power grid adjacent to the school site. There are proposals for air rights projects over the tracks, over the river, in the river or on its banks, reassociating the city with Hispanic Boyle Heights to the east. The opportunity to plan and to build over the tracks, to remake the river, to cross the river, and to connect with east Los Angeles should be integrated with our conception of remaking this city as it moves east — the reverse of that dated sense of Los Angeles that imagined West LA as proprietary.

SCI-Arc is a unique opportunity to reimagine the Arts District with parks, cultural facilities, and high-rise housing looking west to Bunker Hill and east to the LA River. Together, renewed sites east and west of SCI-Arc represent nothing less than the chance to re-conceptualize the east edge of downtown: Through the Arts District, over the tracks, into the river, and on to Boyle Heights.

The antique planning notion that downtown is the east edge of a city that begins at the Pacific Ocean and ends at Grand Avenue is gone. The essential LA is no longer West LA. From the Grand Avenue project, First Street should connect to Alameda and Santa Fe to the east, then south to the SCI-Arc redevelopment zone, so that the twin developments are interdependent. The projects from First and Grand to Third and Santa Fe and on to Boyle Heights over the First Street Bridge will coalesce, thereby ending the era of *hot and cold LA*.

SCI-Arc moved to the old freight depot on Santa Fe in 2000, opening up a downtown front in the fight for an understanding of "contemporary architecture." SCI-Arc can't camouflage its radicalism at the center of that discussion. *The advent of SCI-Arc downtown made a political and policy making extrovert of a once introverted maker of architectural poetry. Reflecting a new maturity, SCI-Arc is now a voice for reimagining the area.*

SCI-Arc has a staff, faculty, and student body of about 550 people. So you can imagine a dilapidated building on Santa Fe, distinguished only by broken bottles and blowing bits of the *Los Angeles Times*, suddenly reinhabited.

A new vision of housing, higher rents, professional services, restaurants, and increased recreational space are a consequence of SCI-Arc's journey to the center of the city. SCI-Arc will draw on the invention and innovation that is part of its history, and the city's tradition of non-tradition in architecture and in planning that runs back to the audacious beginning of the city in the desert.

Lecture, REDCAT (Roy and Edna Disney CalArts Theater), April 12, 2004.

Welcome Back to the Real Forbidden City

Hitoshi Abe

—

Good evening, Mr. Abe. Good to see you in LA, and welcome back to the real Forbidden City.

I think you'll find that the city you left is not the city you've returned to. As you know, Los Angeles began an architecture revolution some years ago. You were a young participant, and I think it's fair to say that the LA revolt ended in unequivocal victory.

What constitutes victory?

Victory means we can now see the built consequences, not only in small experimental structures, but in enormous projects going up around the world today. Victory doesn't necessarily mean that design in Los Angeles has made the world better or worse. What it means is that Los Angeles architecture made the conceptual *pro forma* different. Los Angeles won that battle of poetry and conception and we accept the laurels — for thirty seconds or so.

But the consequences of the battle are a subject for historians, and if there is any durable tradition here, it's that Los Angeles is never a venue for historians. We're architects, and that's not a mere professional designation: It often defines a life.

So what's the LA lesson? Celebrate the victory, but the victory is ephemeral.

And now we come to the next step, and you come to help us with that. I think you'll find the collective mind of Los Angeles substantially more self-conscious about its role in the design discourse than when you first arrived, and that self-consciousness is sometimes bad for our health: Cure it when you find it.

Too much seriousness — what we owe, to whom, who's looking and listening — and we emasculate that exploratory, speculative, often clumsy process of experimentation. You and your generation can continue to remind us that Los Angeles should forever be prepared to stumble, to err, to miss the presumed mark. *The advocacy of that experimental mind set means being comfortable being uncomfortable: That's the enduring tradition of non-tradition.*

Los Angeles, at its best, is less a city of established personalities and more a city where *What else you got?* has an established constituency.

The architecture discourse in Los Angeles, at its best, cares nothing for institutional limits or definitions. Not my school or your school or their school. LA ain't the place for institutional sectarianism. Institutional competition takes us off our subject.

So what's the subject?

Probably easier to define in retrospect. Perhaps if you can name it before you do it then you know it *a priori*, and if you know it *a priori* and can name it, it won't work here.

Ulysses told the Cyclops: "My name is no name." LA architecture has no name, notwithstanding numberless efforts to apply a label. Collaboration, another name for friendship, will be essential. Institutional perimeters — USC, UCLA, SCI-Arc, Art Center — are irrelevant.

In the broadest sense, the condition of the city is the unnamed subject. When you left, LA celebrated architecture as event. *Today, Los Angeles is in the process of defining the constituent parts of a world city: No longer simply the single building, but architecture as a building multiple, and the city as the main event.*

You will recall that Los Angeles architects used to talk exclusively to friends and colleagues at places like the AA and the Bartlett and the ETH. We still do. But now we talk to Mayor Villaraigosa, Councilperson Jan Perry, LA District Attorney Gil Garcetti and developer Eli Broad — and they're listening.

The introverts have become extroverts, without conceding the poetry. You're an aspiring poet: LA welcomes new poetry. You're an urbanist: LA is today, uniquely, a laboratory for urbanism.

Let me make a prediction: Fifteen years from today, you'll be standing on a podium at UCLA welcoming the new director of SCI-Arc to a city which redefined architecture and then, in your time, reimagined the city, and exported that lesson.

Please welcome Hitoshi Abe to Los Angeles.

Introduction to Hitoshi Abe lecture, SCI-Arc, January 31, 2007.

Editor's Note: This lecture was given the same week that Hitoshi Abe assumed the Chair of the Architecture Program at UCLA.

Will We Build Our Cities on the Slopes of Vesuvius?

Jean-Louis Cohen

—

Friedrich Nietzsche, that famous urban strategist, once directed us to "Build our cities on the slopes of Vesuvius."

How is that admonition useful to the history of architecture?

Architecture is often a solitary subject on a long list of solitary subjects. On occasion, architecture trancends its solitary limits and subsumes that long list. When it does, architecture can transform culture. *That means that architecture becomes not simply the confirmation of a broader historic pattern, but the initiator of that pattern.*

The discourse that advances the history of architecture beyond a simple chronology of building is an old one. Its authors are the cartographers of culture, mapping history as best they can, knowing that map will inevitably be redrawn.

We write history, and history becomes the history we write.

And Tolstoy tells us: "History would be an excellent thing if only it were true."

Today, the arbiters of culture are often referred to as historians or theorists or critics.

The best: Mumford debunking the myth of the machine; Nietzsche with his contempt for the flies of the contemporary marketplace; Elias Canetti with his analysis of abusive crowds and power; Thucydides on life and death in Pericles' funeral oration. The best create the narratives we require to manage the world conceptually.

Are these theories intrinsically so? Do they tell us who we are, or do they prescribe our aspirations? Do our options exist only within the history we write, or are there options available to us in the history not yet written? Do we require a chronology, or a sequence, or a cycle to locate ourselves?

In evaluating the origin of Roman cities, Joseph Rykwert once claimed that the Roman who walked the Cardo knew that his walk was the axis around which the sun turned, and that if he followed the Decumanus he was pursuing the sun's daily course. That's a fascinating exegesis of the now ubiquitous urban grid, whose connection to the sun's axis we have surely lost.

Over the last century, this search for the next Cardo has become a more piecemeal endeavor, with a number of independent disciplines — Economics, Sociology, Politics and others — competing for primacy.

Lewis Mumford, lamenting the predictable failure of one of the most promoted and enduring of these hypotheses, catalogs his disappointment with Marx:

> What did not take place in the revolutions of the 20th century was the fulfillment of the romantic fantasy of an instant revolution, a spontaneous transformation from which the new man or the new community or the new world would suddenly appear.

Are Marx's thesis, antithesis, and synthesis still durable prognosticators, or *will we discover a revolution on the slopes of Vesuvius?*

Introduction to Jean-Louis Cohen lecture, SCI-Arc, October 6, 2003.

Delimiting Architecture's Subject Matter

Chris Burden

—

Does architecture belong to a category of defined requirements beyond which it can't proceed, or beyond which, if it proceeds, it becomes something other than architecture, or can architecture be architecture and simply explore what and where it chooses?

... and the obligatory corollary: *When architecture exceeds the exigencies of utility, does it become something called art?*

In a conventional sense, categorical imperatives — art, architecture, and others — belong to a traditional conception of history: The collecting and collating of ways to see, to think, and to understand, and how, over time, the old ways perpetually become new ways.

Suppose the categories were gone: No baroque, no Middle Kingdom, no Third Dynasty; no Marxists, no Toynbeeites, no Freudians; no art, no architecture. Suppose this naming was only an imposition of the most creative labelers, to facilitate a discussion which could be (and will become, in time) any number of other discussions that only await the next imaginative categorical imperative.

In other words, suppose the categories of history are only temporary. Let's consider the possibility that the ongoing metamorphosing of beautiful things is never a sequence or a chronology or a philosophical theory or a system or method of any sort, but simply a numberless series of creative acts that join other such acts across time.

I want to reuse a metaphor from the Swiss architectural historian, Sigfried Gideon, who once referred to the history of artistic creation as a river moving eternally out of the past, into the future, on which creative navigators float their boats. *The river has no end and no begin-*

ning. It simply flows with beautiful things, joined (and separated) by the water in which they sail.

Introduction to Chris Burden lecture, SCI-Arc, April 9, 2003.

Solitary Architecture

Michele Saee

—

There's a propitious New Testament opening that tells us where concepts originate: "In the beginning was the word..." That biblical proposition is probably one that many architects have neglected to read because their work starts from a very different vantage point: "In the beginning is the act..."

In the parlance of contemporary architecture, the conception of buildings belongs to a discourse, and that discourse associates building with any number of hypotheses that precede the act of conception and design. *So the meaning of building inevitably derives, at least in part, from a theoretical discussion, and the building becomes the physical exegesis of that discussion.* In addition, the discourse automatically provides a format for interpretation: The success of the building can be measured in terms of how the project conforms to the tenets of the theory.

For instance, Jean Prouvé and Marcel Lods idealize construction as an industrialized, assembly line sequence of prefabricated parts, which sets the theoretical precedent for an avant-garde building typology.

For Tange, Kurasawa and Kikutake, human physiology suggests a parallel structure for buildings and cities. For the metabolists, the physiological model is the analog for the urban model.

Bauhaus director Hannes Meyer announces that architecture's fundamental equation is "function times economics." So new architecture at the Bauhaus becomes the embodiment of Marxist economic theory, and the *Neue Sachlichkeit* [the New Objectivity] delivers the building.

Look at the painted works of Gris, Braque, and Picasso at the beginning of the 20th century and examine Le Corbusier's plan for Algiers twenty-five years later. Architecture in Algiers becomes the built expression of the cubist painter's ideal.

Then there's the case of the seminal literary figure, Paul de Man, often labeled the inventor of deconstruction. For de Man, there is no single *Moby Dick*. Rather, there are simply multiple Mobys. Ditto, the transmutation from literature to deconstructed architecture, where the demolition of generic space results in an infinite variety of private spatial speculations.

Is there an architecture that belongs to the meanings it alone invents?

Is there an architecture that exists as a critical examination of its own subject matter?

———————

Introduction to Michele Saee lecture, SCI-Arc, November 25, 2005.

The Daedalus Ethos

Steven Holl

—

Today is the eleventh of September, 2003.

For all the destruction on that day two years ago at the end of Manhattan, the possibility of an alternative prospect for architecture continues to resound from that traumatized building site. I don't want to suggest that we have mastered the meaning of that event. *Meaning will depend on what events follow.* But can architects lead what follows?

It seems to me that architecture's insular and often fratricidal debate — the decon, the new urban, the neo-modern, the ubiquitous machine, and so on — must be replaced. A discourse less self-serving is on its way to engage a now enormous and attentive public. Architecture is metamorphosing.

There are those who once imagined history's progression with America standing as the ultimate destination at the end of a teleological line. We must demand a revamped reading of that antique history lesson. What's coming is a new discourse.

There are those who will try to convince us that the world is as it is because it simply couldn't be conceived in any other way. Any instinct to resist, to interrogate, or even to withdraw is consigned to a category of behavior they label "unreal."

But there is always someone who is convinced that the world could be other than it is, could be imagined differently, and is determined to propel it where it needs to go. That means, in concept, that the world is perpetually malleable.

There is a famous description by Ovid of the mindset of Daedalus, the architect of Minos' labyrinth. Trapped on the island of Crete, Daedalus remarked:

> Minos may control the land, Minos may control the sea,
> But Minos does not control the air, So by the air I will go.

(The invention of the wax wings follows.)

What I want to call the "Daedalus Ethos" is emphatically not a signature, or in the current lexicon, a brand. In fact, a brand (a known, *a priori* image) denigrates the originality of conception.

An old friend of Daedalus' once proposed a metaphor for creation and its relationship to the constant need for demolishing precedents. He called it the square with no corners.

The land blocked.
The sea barricaded.
But by air? Minos couldn't anticipate that.

Introduction to Steven Holl lecture, SCI-Arc, September 11, 2003.

Who Rules the Machine?

Wes Jones

—

Single-minded, sometimes powerful, architecture originates in both private, idiosyncratic experiences, and from generic paradigms that attempt to pull the world together and state collectively what the world is and what it might come to be.

From the Gallery of Machines to Marcel Lods and Jean Prouvé, through Peter Cook, Warren Chalk, and Ron Herron, to the Pompidou, Lloyds of London, and the Shanghai Bank building, one finds the chronology of a vision. First tentative, experimental, and unbuilt. Then a competing conception, initially constructed at a small scale in a world that sees it as an unwelcome intrusion and an unfounded speculation; next the construction of larger scale, and finally, huge corporate projects. Through time, a once fragile conception becomes the embodiment of fiscal potency and redefined "progressive imaging."

So which machine are we investigating, the speculative adventure early in the 20th century, or its corporate confirmation at the end?

The machine rules: Does this mean that the machine rules us? That we serve the machine? Or does it suggest that we are about to hear the axiom, the rules by which the machine operates?

Next, are we looking with admiration at the prowess, at the results of the practical application of sophisticated mechanized technique which has allowed us to span rivers, build to the sky, split the atom, fly the continents (and the solar system), and imagine both surgery and war as a long distance video? Or are we looking at the look — the image of the technique and the style of the tools that, as one commentator once noted, "cost $750/square foot to make a museum look like an oil rig in the North Sea?" In other words, are we saying that the image of technique conveys its historic prowess?

It is important to keep in mind that machine history and image are complex and often contradictory. Do we want to represent them selectively?

An anecdotal recollection: In 1979, the American president, Jimmy Carter, sent the most sophisticated of American helicoptering machines to the Iranian desert to rescue Americans imprisoned in the embassy in Tehran. Sand got into the propellers, the mission failed, and the machines, now rusted chunks of steel, were exuberantly displayed by the Iranians. Technique and its missions are not omnipotent.

So the machines, at least on that occasion, belonged to purposes and to a symbolism that is almost absent from the historic architect's advocacy. Le Corbusier's lament: "They build cars on an assembly line; why don't we build houses the same way?" omits a significant portion of a history substantially more complex than the "architecture as a machine for living in" story represents.

Perhaps the question is not whether the machine rules. Rather the question is, who rules the rules of the machine?

Introduction to Wes Jones lecture, SCI-Arc, January 29, 2003.

Architecture of the Up-To-Date

Bill MacDonald

—

Is the work discoursed here the purveyor of a shared ideological conception, or a particular design vision that belongs uniquely to a single architect? Or some of both?

What sort of inquiry would allow us to categorize the work as either introverted single-mindedness, or extroverted collective argument? Or some of both?

Three questions:

First, what is the obligation of design conception to the application of new media in the development of that design?

Second, does the process of invention associate new representational techniques with the development of new construction technologies, or are these two subjects to be understood discretely?

Third, is the design process an enduring belief system or a provisional paradigm?

Meanwhile, there may be another category of investigation, which should precede the above. I am fascinated by the CNN maps where alleged experts move set pieces across modeled topographic surfaces in order to represent military strategy or the movement of troops and machines. Theoretical premises always point to analytical conclusions, and I often wonder whether the individual *qua* individual in the sand and mud is eviscerated by an analytical model of himself as a percentage of a dot or a portion of a line or arrow? I'm not saying that architecture is war. That's a topic for another day. What I am asserting is that history is often written as time generalized, and yet, in the most fundamental sense, life is personal and history can only be made intelligible one life at a time.

So when meanings of architecture are considered, how does the work of any architect conform to or deny a generalized, CNN-like rendition of the history of design? Are the analytical rendition and the individual life model non-sequitors, or are there, perhaps, at least two kinds of history?

To state that architecture confirms a world and its values, or that architecture takes exception to those values, or that architecture propounds alternative values, requires a definition of that world. The defining is somehow history. In particular, *an evaluation of an architect's work requires a conception of the world in which the architecture is conceived, because the work, implicitly at least, claims both to confirm the qualities of a new world view, and simultaneously, to move that view forward.*

A well-known Danish philosopher once admonished that for those who claim to investigate the meanings of human experience, architecture included, the perimeter of discovery is forever limited to what he called the "ground covered by the fathers." In other words, although architects' responses may vary infinitely, the essential subject matter is finite. The discovery process, according to this definition, will always consist of new eyes on an enduring subject. This argument was made in an early 19th century volume by Kierkegaard whose title is also instructive: The *Concluding Non-Scientific Postscript.*

Is it possible that the current argument for the "architecture of the up-to-date" will always and forever be out-of-date? Or, to put it in more tangible terms, *doesn't Brancusi forever render Maya a redundancy?*

Introduction to Bill MacDonald lecture, SCI-Arc, April 2, 2003.

Urban History

Ed Soja

—

In Tolstoy's *War and Peace*, the French face the Russian army at the Battle of Borodino. A bayonetted Russian cavalryman, bewildered in the fog and the smoke of battle, collapses in the sludge along a riverbank.

History is chaos.

A hundred and fifty years later at the Sandhurst military academy, a professor and his students analyze the battle: The cavalry did this, the infantry that; the topography, weaponry, weather, and so on. They map the geography of the battle.

History is conceptual.

Tolstoy's conclusion: History would be an excellent thing if only it were true.

Ed Soja applies the Tolstoy dialectic to the study of cities: One geography or multiple geographies? A single map or innumerable maps? The city experience, one citizen at a time, or the city collective, amenable to empirical analysis?

The hackneyed phrase tells us: "What you see is what you get."

Ed Soja tells us: *"What you get in the city is contingent on what you don't see."*

Ed Soja maps a city's geography, and perhaps the city's geography becomes the geography he maps. Soja delivers an urban exegesis: Origins, transitions, permutations, or cause and effect, or sociolo-

gy and economics, or genuine and disingenuous, or characters, or institutions. No canned allegiances, ideologies, or caricatured villains and heroes.

Ed Soja explains the past to the present and foreshadows the future: Is one city every city? Is there an *a priori* pattern of urban evolution and decline? Does the city belong to its own exigencies, or do the city's causes precede the city itself?

There are two prototypical urban stories. One is simply to extricate an urban narrative, cause and effect, constituent parts, and destination. But what destination? That's option two: Can we manipulate the causes to reformulate the effects to imagine a new and different city?

Does Ed Soja chronicle urban history, or is he an aspiring city architect, speculating on the next metropolis?

Which brings us to Los Angeles. *Does the Soja exegesis anticipate a "future city" not entirely obligated to the intersection of the past and the present, that obviates precedent to create new precedents?* Is Los Angeles that urban surprise?

Ed Soja will tell us.

Introduction to Ed Soja lecture, SCI-Arc, February 28, 2007.

The Real Forbidden City

Thom Mayne/Morphosis

—

Meanwhile at SOM

I remember walking the campus at UC Berkeley in 1968: Long haired students on the march, announcing each *cause célèbre* with kaleidoscopic signage. Two years later, on a sojourn at Skidmore, Owings, and Merrill in San Francisco, I noticed the same long hair, now on the heads of the SOM partners. And around the corner at Macy's, the heretofore raucous graphics metamorphosed on Macy's shopping bags and wrapping paper.

I'm fascinated by the infinitely dexterous and adaptive capacity of American commerce to quickly absorb the appearance of innovation, and by so doing, (perhaps) emasculate the innovator's underlying subversive prospect.

Sinbad the Sailor

A similar cultural metamorphosis is detectable in the recent evolution of the language itself, which fractures when the predictable amalgamation of capital letters, nouns, verbs, and periods is insufficient to communicate (for some poet or other), and tentative new language forms — structure, phrase, vocabulary — emerge: "Sinbad the Sailor, Tinbad the Tailor, Jinbad the Jailer," and so on.

And just as quickly (and surprisingly?), the new is absorbed and becomes, almost seamlessly, a part of the lexicon, with an immediate place in the latest Webster's.

Kafkaesque

This interrogatory speculates on the nature of this now predictable cultural journey, from the precarious acceptance of an original instinct to its broad public acknowledgement. For example: What does the now common usage of the term "Kafkaesque" have to do with *The Trial*; or tabloid journalism's adoption of the "surreal" label to do with the art of Breton, Rothko, or de Chirico?

And a corollary: Does a public ratifying of a poetic insight compromise or abet the poignancy, idiosyncrasy, and contentiousness of the original discovery?

Or, how does the dissemination of an idea affect its depth as it assumes a more "comfortable" place in the cultural lexicon?

The "hate you/love you" case
The architecture rejection/acceptance, instinct/method, "hate you, love you" case adds this essential irony: *Ipso facto,* an architecture initiative requires at least a modicum of public acknowledgment in order to emerge as architecture.

The metamorphosis of Morphosis
Let's use the architect Thom Mayne as the proto-cultural remodeler and the current metamorphosis of Morphosis from relative anonymity to public plausibility as the prototype private-to-public journey.

In the real Forbidden City
Thom's story starts in the world's real Forbidden City, contemporary Los Angeles.

Why is the city significant? It's a relatively young city, and perhaps only relatively a city, so its persona is formative and preliminary (a perfect venue, in retrospect, for Mayne). Los Angeles' reputation as something of an urban experiment is manifest in the city's collective propensity to endlessly but incompletely reimagine itself (again, in retrospect, a perfect venue for Mayne). And this never quite determined city is forever under investigation by a changing cast of civic heroes and villains, including a few who are sometimes both. Thom Mayne is one of those too.

The equivocal city
So the Mayne investigation is synonymous with the advent of an

architect whose experimental form language uniquely character-
izes the equivocal urban experiment that is Los Angeles.

The Mayne experiment resonates publicly because the architecture forecasts the emergence of a particular city at a particular time,
and makes genuinely palpable, spatial, and tactile a physiology, a
persona, an architecture that signifies the conscious arrival of the
city. And all the while, the work retains its subversive, sometimes an-
tagonistic, "in the process of... ," piece by piece character: A puzzle
where the pieces are invented during assembly.

Mayne the two-timer. Exclusively mutual.
Two-timing here was crucial: The extroverted rise of the city, the
introverted growth of the architect. Not mutually exclusive; rather,
exclusively mutual.

The architect had an instinct. It would have been different in a
historic, pedigreed city, but Los Angeles is neither. And as Thom
interrogated the happenstance city, heretofore lacking any iconic speculation on how its evolving definition might translate as
architecture, he began, tentatively at first, to introduce a lexicon, an
image, a spatial strategy, an iconic sensibility that the city's conceptual tensions suggest.

Ringstraße veto
Never a Champs-Elysées, or Ringstraße, or Ramblas, or 5th or
Michigan Avenues, or Red Square... No pedigree derived urbanisms
or the architectural manifestations that inevitably accompany those
histories.

Populist Thom
Thom's initiative is intrinsically populist as it references implicitly
the Forbidden City of the '92 Los Angeles riots: Fire red, then black
smoke and grey concrete. Architecture that is in unresolved tension.
Street corners, freeways, concrete river beds, power grids, abandoned railway tracks, and the apparently endless lateral extension
as the city grows.

But never symmetrically (not the architecture; not the city) — which would indicate a Los Angeles affiliation with a traditional master plan, and an equilibrium or balance, and a mastery of history that, in Thom's rendition, would represent the anticipation of a conclusion Los Angeles should never claim.

Get off at the wrong exit

There's an old Los Angeles joke that you can get off the freeway at the right exit and you can get off at the wrong exit and it doesn't make any difference. It's that LA sense of inconclusiveness and often banal homogeneity, sometimes dark and aggressive, sometimes nonchalant and indifferent, which is very much the sense of the city expressed so succinctly in Mayne architecture.

Simultaneously reticent and confrontational, forbidding, intriguing, welcoming... The architecture delivers an all inclusive emotional gamut in space and surface. And it's absolutely genuine. No punches pulled. We who inhabit the place had an instinct for what the city was; we sensed the city's sense. And when Thom designed it and built it, we saw it and recognized ourselves and our city immediately. Jacob Burkhardt defined and labeled the Italian Renaissance four hundred years after it took place. Ditto Mayne, who didn't wait quite as long to configure the underlying asymmetrical tensions of a city in a perpetual state of becoming. He both founded and expropriated an architecture which belongs to the city, and is the urban epiphany that explains and elucidates it.

LA's stenographer

Mayne, perhaps inadvertently, became LA's stenographer, decoding what the city dictated: "Nobody tells me anything new," said Friedrich Nietzsche, "so I tell myself my own story."

LA is not a city for architecture, though it is a city for architects. You have to look hard and long to locate those special GA [*Global Architecture*] moments amidst the freeways, tracks, tracts, power grids, and momentary high risers. But they're there. And each particular inevitably affirms the Forbidden City as source, a context learned from, that now learns from him.

Mayne as a synonym

Mayne is a double meaning. He's a synonym, a ditto. As he epiphanized and linguistified LA's character, he invented an iconography of his own. It's not the iconography of the ascetic introvert, but the iconography of the populist extrovert. It's not an import from Prouvé or Lods or Le Corbusier or Stirling (although Thom must have looked at all those guys and laughed). Mayne architecture is the architect's transmutation of the homegrown voice of Wilshire and Alvarado. And if LA urbanism is contagious, then the architecture portends a form language suggestive of what might soon be arriving in any number of other cities.

Perhaps this is Los Angeles at its self-confident best: Not much interested in any collected or collective *a priori* allegiances.

The Forbidden City, as Mayne delivers it, is a world intent on creating its own authority. No historic grafting. Thom's work, like the city he taught and learned from, is a race with a moving finish line.

The center and the edge

In a socio-political sense, Mayne architecture won't make the world better or worse. But Thom gave a 21st century city an unvarnished sense of itself, and by building pieces, he built a Mayne lexicon. Thom didn't make the world better or worse; he made it different. He got on the magazine cover, but kept his office in the garage. The edge didn't come to the center as did haircuts at Skidmore or graphics at Macy's.

In Thom Mayne's case, the center went to the edge, where poignancy, idiosyncrasy, and subversion endure.

Morphosis: Volume IV, published by Rizzoli Press, 2006.

A Tale of Two Cities

Stanley Saitowitz

—

Stanley Saitowitz is an architect from San Francisco. Or is he?

There have been numberless attempts over the years, particularly from the literati, to inform us about what Los Angeles lacks, or to suggest what Los Angeles should do to legitimize itself. This arcane debate usually includes recitations of alternative urban models, purporting to exemplify civic beauty among other presumed virtues. San Francisco is often catalogued as one of those beauties.

I want to consider Stanley Saitowitz using the paradigm of two cities in opposition: San Francisco and Los Angeles. I'm less interested in the cities in a literal sense, more concerned with each city as a metaphor for conditions that facilitate or inhibit the advent of new architecture.

If San Francisco were to be assigned an urban persona, it would be one of confidence in its purpose and ultimate value. That prototype is not likely to be receptive to any proposition that the city's future should significantly diverge from its present. That is, the city's successful present is synonymous with the city's successful future. That persona is extremely fastidious about any modifications that imply it should become other than it is. The present will be the future. And this pattern is the definition of entrenched civic conservatism. What happens to the work of an architect who is pressured to conform to this self-satisfied model?

In this parable of two cities, San Francisco is the thesis and Los Angeles the antithesis.

The Los Angeles persona has a more complex definition. *Los Angeles personified is unsure of its ultimate value as a city form. Los Angeles' personality is multiple and evolving.* If schizophrenia is a cure and not a disease, Los Angeles' prognosis is for enduring health.

Paradoxically, the equivocal sense of the contemporary condition mandates the most imaginative speculations on the city's future. In fact, conjecture is the promise of Los Angeles architecture. SCI-Arc has always understood that.

So is it better to reign in the hell of Los Angeles or to serve in the heaven of San Francisco? Stanley Saitowitz knows.

The San Francisco persona is a center, the Los Angeles persona, a perimeter. The center knows; the perimeter wonders. Out on the perimeter, there is a perpetual danger of falling. Relocating to the center, there is a perpetual danger that the edge will disappear.

Stanley Saitowitz appeared on the international scene in the early 1980s with the astonishing flying roof in South Africa, a building that defied every tradition of that traumatized country. Soon after, he departed for San Francisco. Or did he?

So does Stanley Saitowitz belong to Los Angeles or San Francisco? At the risk of revealing his punch line, let me assure you, Stanley Saitowitz is emphatically a Los Angeles architect.

Introduction to Stanley Saitowitz lecture, SCI-Arc, September 24, 2003.

Incomplete In Perpetuity

Tom Gilmore
—

A notorious Danish philosopher once claimed that his day was divided into two parts: Half of the time he would sleep; the other half he would dream.

Little did the man from Copenhagen realize he was anticipating the *modus operandi* of Tom Gilmore, a transplanted New Yorker who has spent at least half of the last ten years dreaming about what downtown Los Angeles might become.

Gilmore isn't an ideologue. He didn't arrive with an a priori *urban theory to implement. He didn't arrive with an obligatory list of the constituent parts of a generic downtown, nor with an interest in reconsidering whether Los Angeles is anti-downtown or not. And he didn't arrive with the intent to polarize LA's long running suburban/urban debate.*

Gilmore landed in the quintessential ephemeral city, a city that continues to reimagine what it is, and willingly explores the possibilities.

LA is incomplete in perpetuity, and that's a perfect Gilmore fit.

No one would hire Tom Gilmore to complete a city. Gilmore belongs to beginnings, to instincts, to intuitions. That's why he's here — less the urban redeveloper, more the urban reinventor.

He is LA's urban performance artist.

Introduction to Tom Gilmore lecture, SCI-Arc, March 2, 2005.

Lexicon

Charles Jencks

—

An 18th century German philosopher once admonished that "From the crooked timber of humanity, no straight thing can ever be made." Immanuel Kant never met Charles Jencks, who for twenty-five years has imposed a variety of precise, analytical models on that crooked timber.

Jencks operates as much like a theoretical chemist as a design critic. He often applies a repertoire of lines, graphs, matrices and other diagrams that systematize, sequence, categorize, and qualify. Charles Jencks, architecture critic, is Charles Jencks, cultural arbiter. In many instances over the years, Jencks has authored the *pro forma* of the architecture/culture discourse. To follow that discussion, a dictionary of Jencks' invented labels is mandatory.

The Jencks lexicon has always been concerned with "naming." As the playwright Shakespeare once reported, "a rose by any other name would smell as sweet." For Jencks, a rose by any other name is an entirely different flora. What are Charles Jencks' most durable conclusions?

The first arrived in a volume called *Modern Movements in Architecture.* Jencks presented us with multivalence, a chemist's label, as a concept for revaluing architecture in the 1970s. *Multivalence deposed the formularized language of modern architecture, and insisted on a more happenstance, less didactic design response in its place.* Jencks proposed the work of James Stirling as the new, multivalent ideal.

Next, Jencks produced *Le Corbusier and the Tragic View of Architecture*, perhaps his most remarkable, and possibly autobiographical text, in which he tied architecture to the Nietzsche of Zarathustra:

"Nobody tells me anything new so I tell myself my own story," says Zarathustra. *The architect creates the culture while attempting to define himself — creation as a synonym for self-examination — watched impassively by a blasé audience.* As Le Corbusier testified: "The architect as acrobat is in perpetual danger of falling" — and the audience doesn't much care.

Jencks' postmodernism provided a conceptual thesis for deconstruction's antithesis which surfaced in the early 1990s — paradoxically, with Jencks' support. Jencks is often both thesis and antithesis.

What does the psychotherapist do with these ongoing theses and antitheses?

For Jencks, it seems the continued production of interpretative cultural regulations is always and forever an act of self-preservation. For all of you who may share the famous acrobat's "perpetual danger of falling," Charles Jencks is about to spread another protective conceptual net.

Introduction to Charles Jencks lecture, SCI-Arc, November 10, 2003.

The Woods Archetype

Lebbeus Woods

—

Here's how the televised advertisement goes: One older man and one younger man stare at what appears to be a maternity room window, each anticipating the arrival of a newborn child to be presented from the other side of the glass. We're not shown what they actually see. At the last moment, the perspective shifts and we understand that the two await not a girl, not a boy, but the arrival of a new Mercedes.

There are those who think life is uniquely personal, meaning each life is its own story, lived one life at a time. There are those who think life is not exchangeable, meaning its lessons are never transferable from one life to another.

Lebbeus Woods' career would seem to confirm both suppositions. And yet a life adventure, idiosyncratic in the extreme, is important to us now because it transcends the personal. Lebbeus Woods is an archetype.

What's the meaning of that assertion? Let's define the archetype anecdotally.

There was a Woods promoted trip to Sarajevo to confront the local politicos with a proposal for an astonishing city planning intervention, the architect's vision for resolving a centuries-old conflict. *Architecture as geopolitical diplomacy.* That's the Woods archetype.

Taut white strings, like wires, ring the Art & Architecture building at Yale and penetrate its volumes from the basement to the sixth floor. Paul Rudolph's design, devoured over the years by innumerable prosaic additions, and Woods' full-scale string installation documenting what had been lost and constructing a poetic case for the resurrection of Rudolph's original. That's the Woods archetype.

And then there was the End of Architecture conference in Vienna, and again, it was Woods applying the politics of pen and ink, insisting not that architecture had ended, or could ever end, or should end, but rather that *architecture was only and always concerned with experimental beginnings.* That's the Woods archetype.

Next, a meeting of architects and planners in Havana, and Woods proposes a kinetic plaza, colossal in scale, that rises to become a protective sea wall along Havana's Malecon waterfront. The plaza, he tells us, is to be constructed as a confirmation of the government's commitment to the democratization of Cuba. That's the Woods archetype.

And now the built versus the unbuilt dichotomy is often alleged as the means to distinguish the constructed real from the unrealized ideal. But is that juxtaposition useful here? Maybe not. Woods continues to elaborate on a consistent and durable series of design and planning ideas which never fail to include the exigencies of building technique and construction. *Not the ethereal unbuilt but the buildable unbuilt.* That's the Woods archetype.

Lebbeus long ago decided, at least implicitly, that he was one who would move the discussion, and the authenticity of the work validates his decision. That's the Woods archetype.

Carl Jung once told us that every human personality is a mixture of two prospects. One he called extrovert, the quality of character which defines itself based on the characteristics of the world it encounters. The other, the introvert, which defines itself based on its private conclusions, unrelated to the world outside itself. *The introvert encounters the world on his own rather than on the world's terms.* Woods is the archetypal introvert.

And finally, "I will forge in the smithy of my soul the uncreated conscience of my race. And I will try to express myself in some mode of life or art as freely as I can and as wholly as I can, using for my defense the only arms I allow myself to use: Silence, exile, and cunning." So said Joyce's Stephen Daedalus. I don't know that Joyce's goal is attainable. But it's the most moving advocacy I know for Daedalus' heroic aspiration. That aspiration also resonates in Lebbeus Woods' voice. That is the Woods archetype. Silence. Exile. Cunning.

Fortunately for the history of our discourse, the smithy is now an architect.

Introduction to Lebbeus Woods lecture, SCI-Arc, February 24, 2003.

The Consummate Engineer

George Yu

—

Dear George,

Nice to see you at SCI-Arc again.

We haven't talked in a few weeks, so I wanted to let you know that I had a chance to visit Shukhov's tower in Moscow the other day which, a little obtusely, suggested some of your recent design adventures to me. The tower is not quite a building, as you probably know. In fact, it resists any conventional nomenclature — like a lot of your work. I guess in the current lexicon, it could be called a "folly" or an "installation," but it's too wrist-cuttingly serious for those labels. I'm not quite sure you're a card-carrying wrist-cutter yet, but it looks like you might be headed there.

The tower is the epiphany of an absolutely unique era of design exploration. I'm hoping it's enduring, but we know how delicate Lenin's steel sections are. So, for all of the usual talk about the durability of building, we both know how precarious, how fragile these results are; and fragility is certainly your subject as well. We've been taught to call the tower "constructivism" not to be confused with its step-sister "deconstruction," which as we both know, has very particular psychotherapeutic problems. Psychotherapy is probably not your area of specialization either, but I think it's fair to say, for your adherents, the work has a positive salutatory therapeutic aspect.

The tower was built in the 1920s, a period of time which continues to inspire because it posits the promise of a colossal re-imagining of how the built world might be redefined as Architecture (unsophisticated though we may be). But to be empirically fair, history also carries the tensions between what we dream and what we realize, and, as we've discussed, sometimes the contradictions tantalize and frustrate and then it all comes out of the ground in Moscow or Guangzhou or Los Angeles. And, as you well know, the results confirm both the toughness of the game and the triumph of achievement, and your work carries the tension of those contradictions.

What was essential to Shukhov — and what, in a different form, I've always associated with your work — was the integration of a social perspective with investigations of technique, fabrication, engineering, and aesthetic vision. The Russians continue to call Shukhov an engineer, and in that sense, you're on the way to becoming the consummate engineer.

I introduced a friend of ours at a lecture the other day, and it was not so much the work that was intriguing as his conclusion, so I want to repeat it: He concluded simply by saying (and he's 75 years old), "I'll see you all in five years and my work will surprise you... Count on that." I want to say the same to you, George: I expect to introduce you again in five years, and the SCI-Arc community anticipates that the spirit of your work will continue to make the discourse dance. Be advised, your next lecture is on the SCI-Arc calendar.

All the best to you and your family,

Eric

Introduction to George Yu lecture, SCI-Arc, September 28, 2005.
Editor's note: George Yu passed away on Saturday, July 7, 2007.

The Psychologist

Shigeru Ban

—

Karl Jung, the Swiss psychoanalyst, identified two personality pro-totypes: The extrovert and the introvert. The introvert bases his life entirely on the internal meanings he alone describes, while the extrovert's frame of reference belongs entirely to the world outside himself.

Jung might be surprised to find his analytical model of personalities applied to the contemporary discourse on architecture:

Let's identify the current internationalist paradigm as a global ex-trovert, and the insular, centuries-in-the-making traditions of Japan as the indigenous introvert. *So Jung's archetypal personality conflict could be imagined not as an exchange within a single individual, but as an intersection of two cultures.*

The architecture of Shigeru Ban, I think, belongs particularly to this tension between competing cultural prospects.

Predictably, the exporting cultural extrovert subsumes the some-times fragile antecedents that belong to the local introvert.

But Shigeru Ban has a more resilient case history.

Admiral Perry, the prototype Western extrovert, sailed into Tokyo Bay in the middle of the 19th century and precipitated a cultural schism that endures today: Can contemporary Japan promulgate what is uniquely and quintessentially Japanese, or should Japan remodel itself in accord with the Western dictionary definition of national priorities?

For Shigeru Ban, neither option entirely solves the architect's problem.

The Swiss/Frenchman, Le Corbusier, a well-known extrovert, built a museum on a hill in Ueno Park, overlooking Tokyo. Kunio Mayekawa and Junzo Sakakura absorbed the French modernist precedent and passed that conceptual *pro forma* on to Kenzo Tange, Kisho Kurasawa, and Kiyonori Kikutake, who in turn handed it to Fumihiko Maki and Arata Isosaki, and on to Toyo Ito and Tadao Ando. Quite an astonishing lineage.

Shigeru Ban observed all this, but refused to swear allegiance to the modernist ideogram. Ban is not the latest link in the Ueno Park lineage. His work suggests a more intricate and contradictory sensibility, one that might belong to the remarkable 7th century Taoist Ise Shrine. At Ise, a building is constructed on one of two adjacent sites and stands for twenty years. The contiguous site remains empty. After twenty years, the building is demolished and an identical structure is built on the adjacent site, and it, in turn, stands for twenty years, and so on and so on. *So the current structure at Ise is always both old and new; forever built, forever unbuilt, forever building; assembling and disassembling; enduring and ephemeral; temporary and permanent; specific and generic; tangible and abstract.*

Shigeru Ban is his own psychologist. As at Ise:

> Ban space,
> Ban shape,
> Ban material,
> Ban detail.

Transform the dated extrovert/introvert dialectic and make Ban architecture a synthesis: Neither the international nor the indigenous allegiance, but a transcendent poetic voice which simultaneously invokes both Jung's prototypes and belongs to neither.

Introduction to Shigeru Ban lecture, SCI-Arc, November 21, 2005.

Tactility

Toshiko Mori

—

An art historian's anecdote tells us that Mies was removed from the CIAM [Congrès Internationaux d'Architecture Moderne] in 1928 because he insisted on using silk in the Barcelona Pavilion. Soft and sensual was never a conceptual fit in early modern architecture's *pro forma*.

And Toshiko Mori edited a book called *Immaterial Ultramaterial*. It's not clear whether this title means that sophisticated new materials are irrelevant, or alternatively, that we're about to review a catalog of materials from the most ethereal to the technologically extreme. Or both. We'll see.

But how is the story of Mies' alleged material violation and his subsequent "excommunication" from the International Congress of Modern Architecture germane to this evening's discourse on materials?

My intention is not to attack Mies or his genre. It is, however, to critique the intellectual foundation of that genre and, by implication, to comment on the fixed perimeter of all such genres. *Architecture's rule systems inevitably form an ideological perimeter, and inevitably leave something outside it. What's fascinating is that what's missed seems always to find a crack in the `dogma, and out of the crack a new voice sometimes emerges.*

Toshiko Mori may be one of those new voices, the spokesperson for the missing CIAM silk.

The advocacy of Toshiko Mori suggests to me a 19th century Seurat painting called *Sunday in the Park.* The setting on the bank of the

Seine is serene, even placid. Sociologically, everyone is properly at-tired and properly disposed. The politics appear to be traditional, neat and in place. No revolution here. But wait a (surreptitious) mo-ment. Let's examine the technique, the assembly: Dots and points. The method for representation is radical and unprecedented, a new way to delineate shape and color, and therefore a new materiality in paint.

Sunday in the Park is an intellectual's case for not making an intel-lectual's case, a painter's argument for sensual experience. From Toshiko Mori, we are likely to hear that the architect's first impetus is not cerebral, not an order, not a method. All those tactics arrive later.

This is what I think gives her work both its poignancy and its new perimeter. *It's not "in the beginning was the word" (or the thought) — which might seem a perfect fit given Toshiko's academic proclivities — but "in the beginning is tactility."*

Paradoxically, words are used here to provide an exegesis for what is not in essence verbal. The new axiom will be "in the beginning are the senses, the poetry." A new material dialectic can follow.

Introduction to Toshiko Mori lecture, SCI-Arc, February 17, 2003.

The Indoorsman

Aaron Betsky

—

Some of you may remember Aaron Betsky as a young architect working and teaching in Los Angeles not so long ago. And some of you will recall Aaron Betsky curating exhibits, writing books, and directing design at San Francisco MOMA. And currently, many of you know Aaron Betsky as the director of design at the NAI in Rotterdam: Entrepreneurial advocate for design, exhibitor, more publications, and a promoter of new architecture in symposia and competition juries around the world.

The next performance venue on Aaron's travel itinerary has yet to be confirmed, but one thing his history suggests: There will certainly be a next venue. Perhaps several. Maybe Los Angeles is in line for a return visit.

What do multiple international stops reveal about this traveler? Students of literature will recognize a narrative form called the picaresque. Characters in a picaresque novel go from adventure to adventure, but there is no continuous storyline. The reader can begin at the end, end at the beginning, or start in the middle. And every chapter is a plausible end or a conceivable beginning. So it is with Aaron. Betsky's career is a picaresque adventure.

I want to briefly define Aaron's role as an international arbiter of design. There are those who tell us that Aaron Betsky is a man without a theory. There are those who tell us that Betsky is a man of many theories. There are those who tell us that Aaron moves from one theory to the next.

I have a different explanation: Ovid, writing two thousand years ago, pinpointed the essential problem with theories of theory. He said:

"What was once impulse, becomes method." *That is, what was initially impulsive inevitably becomes method over time. Impulse leads creation; impulse confounds theory; impulse is pre-theory/pre-method — the prognosis of a journey with the destination still in doubt.* Betsky understands this instinctively.

By the time theory arrives, the precariousness of instinct has been supplanted by a rule system; from the fragility of impulse to the weight and rigor of theory. But Aaron's not waiting for weight. He has moved on.

Betsky is Kafka's famous indoorsman, fishing in a bathtub where there are no fish, and expecting to land a whale (and sometimes, he does).

Aaron's work continues to stretch the boundaries of the design discourse. He has become a discoverer of discoverers, and this is a rare talent. He locates those instincts likely to move the culture and supports them. His objective is not to make the culture better or worse, but to make it different. He is a progenitor of change.

Thucydides got it about right when describing the Betsky type: "...He was born never to live in peace and quiet himself and to prevent the rest of the world from doing so."

Introduction to Aaron Betsky lecture, SCI-Arc, September 17, 2003.

Multiple-Choice Career

Michael Sorkin

—

There's an old Spanish proverb which reads as follows: "Tell me to what you pay attention and I'll tell you who you are." The proverb presumes that each human life demands choices, and that an evaluation of choices made reveals the intrinsic meaning of that life. This premise obviously requires that some options and opportunities will be ruled out and others in.

Now we come to the human anomaly known as Michael Sorkin, whose personal and professional bibliography seems directed at emasculating the proverb's premise, *because what is most intriguing about Michael's career is that he seems to have ruled everything in.* This is, of course, not literally true, but perhaps it is asymptomatic to the truth.

Michael continues to teach and to lecture from nearly every available podium on the planet. He speaks about cities and buildings. He advocates. He pillories.

Michael continues to write, to editorialize and to edit: Books, magazines, newspapers — print and electronic — on issues social, political, and economic. Michael is less polemicist, more polemicists. And we're not done yet.

Michael makes exhibits and installations. He continues to propose city plans and building projects. And he is heard and listened to, though to be fair, not everyone is a subscriber.

So, how can we tell Michael who he is?

There have been frequent discussions of the division of knowledge into discrete categories, of the compartmentalization of ideas, and the rise of specialists who talk only to other specialists as they congratulate each other on the wisdom they alone share.

That conception of knowledge is the antithesis of Sorkin's. Michael breaks down conventional intellectual and professional categories. *He reconciles and reassociates disparate areas of knowledge. He returns us to a literate and integrated conception of human affairs, far from the prevailing segregated model. And for this, he has been criticized for dividing himself too thinly.*

Michael Sorkin's ecumenical ambitions are unique in the contemporary discourse of architecture. But not everyone has the versatility or the stomach for a multiple-choice career. So, in the most supportive and empathetic sense, I want to recite for Michael a refrain I recall from a sign over the entrance to a cemetery in Genoa:

"Congratulations and Condolences."

Introduction to Michael Sorkin lecture, SCI-Arc, November 6, 2002.

The Builder

Frederick Fisher

—

There are architects who tell us that architecture is not architecture unless it's art. There are architects who claim that architecture is simply architecture and requires no further qualification. There are artists who say that art is for artists only, and the prosaic subject matter of architecture *ipso facto* doesn't qualify. And finally, there are a few artists who insist that their art is, in fact, architecture.

We won't resolve these differences today, but the resolution will lie not in the nuances of argument or the intellectualization of the terms "art" and "architecture," but always in the act of building. And since building follows building, that resolution is forever in transit.

Fred Fisher has invented a unique Los Angeles practice. And the essential meaning of that practice lies in his efforts to intervene definitively in the art/architecture discourse.

There are projects where Fred appears simply as a thoughtful facilitator of the exhibition of art, the production of art, the warehousing, maintenance, and repair of art, and the education of artists. There are projects where Fred clearly asserts the independence and priority of architecture, distinct from its responsibilities to facilitate the art. And there are occasions where the architect builds a complex interrelationship between contradictory poetic and accommodation priorities, without indicating a preference for either.

Perhaps the aggregate is Fisher's discovery. *His authorship is hybrid, not singular; shared rather than insular; more collective than idiosyncratic; more social than privately existential. For Fisher, the meaning of the art/architecture hybrid is forever plural.*

Introduction to Frederick Fisher lecture, SCI-Arc, February 2, 2005.

The Stanley Doctrine

Stanley Tigerman

—

Once upon a time in the city of Chicago, Stanley Tigerman designed a library for the blind and the handicapped. Two elevations were plastered. The third side in the triangular plan was a poured concrete wall, 250 feet long and 20 feet high, punctured by an elongated glazed opening with a cosine curving head. According to Tigerman, Mayor Daley signed on to provide the extra cash to construct the wall in a single pour. So the wall was poured, the forms were stripped, Tigerman took a look, couldn't stomach the result, rejected it, and painted the wall grey.

Stanley Tigerman grew up as a technical virtuoso, an inheritor of a form language passed along from Marcel Lods, John Prouvé, 860 Lake Shore Drive, Yale, Rudolph, and that ubiquitous hundred year pedigree of Chicago construction experiments. *Suddenly, instead of ratifying Chicago architecture's mid-20th century techno* pro forma, *Stanley disowned it, and painted the wall.*

That "paint it" decision may seem insignificant in today's discourse, but at the time it was a radical conceptual choice. By painting a 250 foot long hunk of surcharge, single pour, board formed concrete, Stanley challenged a governing structural/material tenet of modern architecture and initiated, along with several others, the "what's next?" discussion that continues today.

Stanley has been one of architecture's agnostics ever since.

I remember sitting on a jury, surrounded by the usual esoteric commentary, and Stanley turned to the group and announced, "I get my lines from Chicago cab drivers." Somewhere between facetious and genuine, Stanley was admonishing his colleagues to drop what he considered to be the pretensions of the discussion, and to move the debate to the more pragmatic constraints of the local street corner. In retrospect, the "I learn from cabbies" remark suggested yet another career course correction for Tigerman.

From confirmed modernist to postmodern agnostic to street corner populist.

Tigerman offered a seminar at the University of Illinois in which students were required to impersonate a renowned philosopher drawn from Stanley's list of accredited intellectuals. One learned student-philosopher debated another; each argued a conceptual position which somehow implicated architecture.

During a studio critique one afternoon, Tigerman suddenly insisted that Mies van der Rohe was actually a classicist; I argued that Mies was a modernist. In the long established tradition of that studio, the student audience demanded a Tigerman/Moss debate. With Tigerman, there's no event without the requisite punishment and reward. Ergo, after each session, the audience vote designated a winner and a loser.

First came the tripartite, classically divided, high-rise Mies, versus the hang the custom five inch by eight inch bronze I-section on the window wall of Seagram Mies. Next, the free form, Friedrichstraße Mies versus the bilaterally symmetrical Lake Shore Drive Mies.

And then they voted.

Over the last thirty years, the Tigerman persona has been one of the most provocative in world architecture. *The Stanley doctrine was never doctrinaire.* Instead, it always seemed multiple, offering a perpetual tension between alternative points of view: The Yale highbrow and the street corner cabby; the doctrinaire modernist and the postmodern agnostic; design *über alles* and a populist conscience.

There's an old Sigfried Gideon metaphor that imagines the history of architecture as a stream flowing from the past to the future, and the best an architect can do is to drop his boats into that stream and see what sinks and what floats forward.

Uniquely among architects, Stanley has dropped a flotilla into that stream, and it wouldn't be a surprise to see a number of those barges docked somewhere upriver, far into architecture's future.

Introduction to Stanley Tigerman lecture, SCI-Arc, March 8, 2006.

Crooked Timber

Mack Scoggin and Merrill Elam

—

The sign posted on the wall of the Lone Star Café in New York City in 1975 reads: "Too much ain't enough."

Two hundred years earlier, Immanuel Kant told us that "From the crooked timber of humanity no straight thing can ever be made."

As disparate as the origins of these quotations appear to be, I'd like to propose that duet as the epigram to the architecture of Mack Scoggin and Merrill Elam.

There are some who might be offended at the use of a catalog of weapons as a means to reveal the spirit of the Scoggin/Elam practice. Nevertheless, one could imagine, for example, the blunt single-mindedness of the architecture of the bomb, or the sporadic but incisive burst of the architecture of the pistol. *How about the surreptitious architecture of the stiletto? It's the weapon of surprise. It's danger incarnate. And it's silent: The act, not the word.* Subterfuge and misdirection are accomplices in the Scoggin/Elam studio of the stiletto.

No weaponry analog alone is sufficient to convey the intent of this architecture. There are, of course, analytical *pro forma* that routinely serve as explanations of an architect's work and facilitate conventional comparisons to the work of other architects. But *pro forma* parallels are inadequate here. Because from architect to architect, projects are organized similarly, but appear differently; projects are materially identical, but differ formally; projects appear similar but organizationally diverge. So a precise definition of the categories for comparison can be so obtuse that the basis for compassion is lost.

Where might we find it?

First, there's the architecture of the ideologues, those who continue to produce according to *a priori* rules. Scoggin and Elam are not ideologues.

Next, there's the architecture of revolution: No rule, the rule; no method, the method; no system, the system. We won't find Mack and Merrill here either. Although perhaps once...

And then there is politics as architecture's surrogate: Architecture is sustainable and green, or the constructed manifestation of a perceived social virtue, or it's not architecture. We'll have to look elsewhere for Scoggin and Elam.

Last, there is the architecture of the non-believers: Sorting through the ideals, but without the ideologues' zealotry. The architecture of the non-believer doesn't necessarily get better (or worse). But it necessarily gets different. And here we find them:

Too much crooked timber from Scoggin and Elam absolutely ain't enough.

<hr />

Introduction to Mack Scoggin and Merrill Elam lecture, SCI-Arc, October 8, 2003.

Double-Headed Whole

Ricardo and Victor Legoretta

—

Several years ago, some friends of mine returned to Los Angeles from Mexico City with a large print of a famous David Alfaro Siqueiros mural. The painting is a Mexican history lesson: A colossal, hybrid head, part Indian, part Spaniard. The two heads intersect without either head conceding any aspect of its own identity, with one astonishing exception: A portion of each head has disappeared, to be replaced by the contradictory portion of its historic opposite.

Two contending realities: The double head confirms a perpetually divided personality, split between two contradictory pasts.

Which pasts? Half is Teotihuacan, Tenochtitlan, Chichen Itza, and Uxmal: Several thousand years of unprecedented Maya, Aztec, and Olmec invention, culture, art, and war. The other half is Spain, the European constituent: The Catholic Church, culture and colonization, and war in the old world and the new.

Two halves and an irreconcilable whole.

So what's the long-term psychotherapeutic prognosis for Mexico's personality split? Let me suggest that new art has the capacity to resolve old history, and to unify the heretofore divided Mexican psyche.

The double face is a question and an answer. The split doesn't disappear in an intellectual response to a historic polemic, but in the breezeways at Ricardo Legoretta's Camino Real Hotel in Mexico City, or in the forever overflowing, but never quite flooding fountain by Luis Barragan at the chapel for Carmelite nuns in Mexico City.

Poetry rewrites history. Architecture can do that as well.

In the 1930s and 1940s, Mexico began to heal that profound Indian/ Spaniard cultural divide. A new form language transformed those previously segregated components in the writings of Octavio Paz, the paintings of Diego Rivera, Jose Clemente Orozco, Siqueiros, and Frida Kahlo, and the architecture of Barragan and Legoretta. Literature, art, and architecture reimagined the old bipolar history.

When we see the work of the Legorettas, we see the aesthetic resolution of Siqueiros' collision of histories:

Building as movement, but not at high speed. Building as enduring weight: Lean on the walls, the walls lean back. Never building as ethereal, never just off the computer screen. Rather, building as palpable surface, color, and material. More raw, less polished.

Siqueiros' dualism was an opportunity for the Legorettas, and they exploited it. *The architects' cure is never discoverable in the intellectualization of conflicting arguments, but in the force and subtlety of the art form that both delivers the conflict conceptually and supersedes it poetically.*

Siqueiros painted the historical dialectic; the Legorettas are building the architectural synthesis. Architecture makes the two heads one.

Introduction to Ricardo and Victor Legoretta lecture, SCI-Arc, October 19, 2005.

Trajan versus Nero

Preston Scott Cohen

—

Recently, I was in Italy to deliver a lecture to Rome's Society of Architects. I was invited to visit Nero's Domus Aurea, now buried in the hill overlooking the Colisseum. What fascinated me was less what Nero had done than the intersection between Nero and his successor, Trajan, whose structure was violently deposited over, around, and through the Domus Aurea below.

I raise this antecdotal piece of history as both a good and bad conceptual example of Preston Scott Cohen's current subject matter, expressed so articulately in drawing over the past several years.

The Trajan/Nero case was not simply the cultural intersection of alternative spatial demands. Rather, it was (for Trajan at least) a personally assertive political act. One can speculate abstractly on the now distilled spatial consequences, but it is more important to understand that Trajan's intention was not intellectually speculative or private. It was of the world, pragmatic, and extroverted. This is an intersection whose objective was to emasculate the form of its predecessor.

The question for Preston Scott Cohen is whether what he presents here is an introverted system, a private cerebral logic which exists either to discover ways of making space, or (equally plausible) to confirm an *a priori* conception.

Does Scott know where he will end up when the process begins, or is the drawn result a perpetually evolving speculation?

Is this a Wittgenstein discussion — an inquiry that arrays spatial formulae against itself while searching for an internal validation? Is the drawing the object of its own predefined subject? Can this be a search that admits other participants?

Could a wall like Steven Holl's Vierendeel wall at MIT come out of a process like Scott's? Recall the improvised stiffner panels that were added where stresses in the truss were extreme. Recall the colored stress diagrams made by the engineer, which suggested the colored interior frames to the architect.

The intriguing question at MIT (or in Trajan's exorcising of Nero), or in Scott's work, is one of the admissability of contradictory obligations, and the possible integration of those contradictions in the *parti.*

To synopsize, here are two bipolar pairs to consider:

One: Drawing as a manifestation of an introvert's system of logic, or drawing as an extrovert's acknowledgement of pressures that can supersede that inner logic.

Two: Drawing as the validation of an *a priori* spatial destination, or drawing as a process of perpetual discovery.

Conclusion and solution: *A priori*, or to be discovered?

Does the purity of Scott Cohen's effort demand one alternative and deny the other?

Introduction to Preston Scott Cohen lecture, SCI-Arc, November 4, 2002.

"Untimely" Urban Meditation

Vittorio Lampugnani

—

Vittorio Lampugnani tells us he intends to deliver an "untimely" urban meditation.

But of course we all understand that "untimely" means precisely the opposite. It means relevant, and perhaps mandatory.

"Untimely" also implies that the message may not conform to the audience's *a priori* urban model, so the audience may be unwilling to listen. "Untimely" posits rejection, but maybe we'll surprise him.

Leo Tolstoy once told us: "History would be an excellent thing if only it were true."

But Vittorio Lampugnani never subscribed to that existential premise. He will tell us that his subject is the history of the city, but that's not quite so either. *His object is the city, but his subject is the poetry of meanings manifest in the evolving physiology of the city.* He is prepared to tell us where we are and why. But he is also prepared to suggest where else we might be and how we might arrive at that destination.

Lampugnani belongs to the "difficult to group" group of critical thinkers over the last hundred years or so who insist that civilization means urban civilization, from Spengler and Toynbee to Mumford, Rykwert, and Isaiah Berlin, those whose discourse is never complete without the admonition that we revalue our values.

Ortega y Gassett often recited a famous Spanish proverb: "Tell me to what you pay attention and I'll tell you who you are." I think Vittorio is about to tell us that our attentions are misdirected.

For Lampugnani, the urban construct is the aggregate of physiological and psychological precedents. So, *ipso facto, the city gives back to us what we are, what we were, and carries a prognosis of what we might become.*

Vittorio's subject is the transformation of meaning in the city, and that meaning defines the substance of collective and individual urban life.

Here's Vittorio's apprehension: That the misplaced clamor for the digital city — the alleged progressive — will emasculate the city he says "carries the great memory of mankind," that was largely a product of the industrial revolution.

Brand identity threatens personal identity. Lampugnani quotes Victor Hugo on the relationship between machine printing and architecture: "This will kill that," i.e., the virtual kills the tactile. He decries what he calls "the vulgar, corporate identity city" and the arrival of "corporate-centric" meaning.

Although he expresses an optimism about our capacity to confront the digital city, he questions our will to power a viable alternative.

We welcome Vittorio Lampugnani's timely proposition.

Introduction to Vittorio Lampugnani lecture, SCI-Arc, March 1, 2006.

An(other) Pro Forma

Johnson Fain

—

There are two theories of evolution. One is Darwin's: Gradual change over long periods of time. The other is cataclysmic: Radical change in an instant.

There are two theories of tradition. One: That the value of the past obligates the conduct of the present and mandates the future. Two, an unorthodox view: That a tradition of non-tradition, the opposition to precedent, is also a route to the future.

SCI-Arc values a critical discourse. But we have to be extremely careful that SCI-Arc doesn't simply insist on its own model for change in the world as we define change, and disregard possibilities that fall outside our formulation.

It's possible to argue that a piece of the "What is architecture and who says so" debate is sometimes missed here. For instance, Ed Soja spoke about a conception of space in the city that he claimed was beyond the purview of most architects. Likewise, the architecture and city planning of Scott Johnson and Bill Fain are also outside the typical, non-traditional SCI-Arc *pro forma*. But that doesn't mean Scott and Bill might not enlarge on the SCI-Arc model.

SCI-Arc architects are often advocates of radical change. Many of the architects who teach, exhibit, and lecture here have pushed architecture to impressive, expressive extremes. The implied, not always articulated, objective is to make architecture different; and indeed to use architecture to imagine another, perhaps superior world. "The world could be other than it is" is the mantra: Let's make it so. And aspiring to make the world different means to confront existing conditions in the world as we find them, or to withdraw from those conditions, or, on occasion, both.

Shock is also a premise, often unspoken, that underlies radical architecture.

The world as intrinsically strange. Or is it?

Johnson and Fain have disowned shock and incorporated Darwin: No to confrontation. No to withdrawal. Surprise is rarely a part of the repertoire, and for them, the world ain't strange. For Johnson and Fain, the world of architecture is a relatively congenial venue.

The Johnson Fain design process is tactical: Less single-minded, more broad-minded. Less categorical, more categories. Less "mine," more "ours."

So the Johnson Fain *pro forma* provokes the most fundamental conceptual question: If the world runs on nihilistic madness, even if the world runs on nihilistic madness, why should architecture confirm that deconstructed vision? Why not an alternative?

Johnson Fain have produced a substantial alternative portfolio of planning and building projects around the world over the last twenty years. Practical, pragmatic, utilitarian, and facile, their work is both studied and learned.

Johnson's recent book, *The Big Idea*, is filled with recitations of buildings and projects, both current and historic. Clearly, the firm's work sits on a solid intellectual premise, with an instinct for the varied traditions that have described the architecture ideal over time.

Minus the shock and awe quotient, one finds a presentation of the Darwinian case for architecture and city planning by Scott Johnson and Bill Fain.

Introduction to Scott Johnson and Bill Fain lecture, SCI-Arc, March 14, 2007.

9.11

RoTo Architecture

—

I remember a couple of Biennales back, walking with Michael Rotondi to look at a huge chunk of ex-World Trade Center steel, now burnt, bent and rusted, that was on display in front of the American Pavilion in Venice, Italy. It was a Barnum & Bailey event, accompanied by a number of drawn prognoses forecasting the future of the site at the end of Manhattan. The exhibition had (nominally) to do with the events of 9.11, but it seemed to us to reflect an *a priori* obligation (perhaps premature) to comment, to explain, and to understand... and to act.

I'm not prepared to announce the historic consequences of the fall of the WTC, but I recall another discourse on history in which Henry Kissinger allegedly asked Chou En-lai what he thought of the French Revolution, and Chou is supposed to have answered, "I don't know... not enough time has passed yet." The (presumed) inevitability of America *über alles* — "History is over (and America's the victor)" — is wobbling. *The whole Trade Center event requires a period of introversion, reflection, patience, even quiet, in order to reimagine the contemporary American experience again in the language of building.*

There is, as yet, no form language to communicate that 9.11 "trauma to the ethos," unprecedented on American soil. And this is one reason why the insistence on remaking the New York site has also wandered, unsure of its purpose, obligated by a need to exhibit a reflexing of the muscles, so the world would know the muscles remain operational. That American capacity to flex tumbled on 9.11, and for architects and others who follow and record the adventures of architecture in the world today, the collapsed twin sarcophagi also brought down much of the form language that partnered with the existential musings of Sartre, Genet, Camus, Ionesco, and de Man:

Pieces but no wholes; the falcon/falconer disconnect, and so on.

There's another frequently argued design polemic that was emascu-
lated at the WTC: 9.11 said good-bye to advocates of technique and
progress, manifest in the language of the assembly line and oil rigs
in the North Sea — the positivist's science and the tools of technol-
ogy as both the (erstwhile) prognosis of our future and the literal language of that future: Steel, the means; steel, the end. *And then there
was all that steel; that bent positivism; that dismantled prowess; that
abused technique (buildings and planes) at the end of Manhattan.*

There we were, staring at that bent chunk that seemed to signify
the end of the positivist/techno advocacy, and the hide and seek aesthetic. Those once poetic idealizations that are now visible through
the fractured aperture of 9.11... Can we make it new?

Introductory essay written for *RoTo Architecture: Still Points,* published by
Rizzoli Press, 2006.

Origins: The World Trade Center
—

Building projects of consequence require a gestation period so that sufficient time is available to hypothesize and reconsider conceptual strategies. Not so the World Trade Center. The WTC is a conceptual non-sequitor in every conceivable way. The felling of the buildings remains a shock and a horror — although the sharpest pain has a way of gradually diminishing, replaced by a dull gnawing and perpetual hurt.

The fog of the World Trade Center
What is the project? Is there a historical antecedent? Is there an American historical antecedent? In a fundamental sense, we don't know the problem, or at least, we didn't know and can't know its ultimate extent. So we will begin to articulate possible solutions as we begin to articulate possible problems — a unique way to think and understand. We don't know and can't guess what transpires next.

If nothing, if never again is a monument, or bridge, or power station, or federal or commercial facility attacked and demolished, then the unique horror remains simply that, an anomaly in an otherwise undisturbed, heretofore self-assured, confident self-image. The stable, renewable American vision of America might perhaps endure.

Pandora's hope
The WTC as historic anomaly is an unlikely hope. How will Americans live their lives, solve day-to-day problems, do business (as usual) in a post-Verdun, post-Bella Wood, post-Iwo Jima, post-Inchon and now post-WTC world? The WTC wrenched the collective American psyche from the conviction that history's pattern is ours to orchestrate. Now we know (not just theoretically, but tangibly) there are opposing initiatives that can harm us. We don't know precisely who

will deliver these, so the mounting of a successful counterattack is obviated. Who should we attack? When and where? When we attack our enemy here, is there another somewhere else? Can we see to the end of this history? We once envisioned history's progression with America standing at the end of that teleological line. Now, the battlefield is infinite, the enemy obscure, and the time line undetermined. *Where are these sensibilities in the WTC program?*

Is the American mission durable? Is the American psyche reparable? Both will have to be revamped to include a revised conception of the precariousness of our reading of history, and the prospect that that fragility will be a perpetual component of the American ethos. *Where is this revamping in the WTC program?*

No one knows yet what to construct on the WTC site. And it is possible that whatever the conception, the result may appear limited to our time — insufficiently deep or broad enough for all time. Perhaps we can't see far enough or extend ourselves past the trauma. It's too enormous and inhibits our consideration of other prospects. These will arrive (perhaps later). *Where is this time-circumscribed perspective in the WTC building program?*

But we can begin to set priorities. That is, we can suggest organizational options to consider, and prospects we might avoid. The solution to the WTC project is not a design signature in the recognizable architectural sense. In fact, a design signature, (a known, *a priori* image) denigrates the originality of conception. This project can't be one of a series. The event and its (re)built response should be unique. *A priori* imaging, however sophisticated in the annals of architecture, would link the project to a pedigree it doesn't share.

"The business of America (was) business"

Any planning and design solution must acknowledge two essential and contradictory tendencies. And both should be part of a statement of the problem. The two possibilities exist dialectically. The concept must recognize both, diminish neither, and simultaneously remake the two.

Can that be done?

First, the primal instinct, often voiced when facing trauma or pain (collective or individual), is to return to normalcy. (Normalcy here means the state preceding the trauma.) At the WTC site, this inclination has a fundamental mercantile aspect. Should the solution suggest a return to an office and commercial site? Should we show our toughness here? "They" knocked it down; we'll show "them;" put it back up; let's do business — business not *qua* business, but big business as America's symbol of big normalcy (which the original building certainly was). But a new commercial life on the WTC site cannot simply validate our old urban land use economic *pro forma*, e.g. five buildings are more efficient than two; fifty floors are more readily leasable/require less vertical circulation than a hundred and ten.

No return to that. The long practiced, simply mercantile voice no longer resonates. But that impulse, the need to rediscover the old voice (best left unrequited), remains alive in many of us. We must say no to that impulse, and demarcate unequivocally the hurt. We won't turn away from what we saw. We'll put it down for those who are here and for those who will arrive later. The horror and the pain, as the instinct to bury them both, demand a tangible form. *Where is this dialectic in the WTC building program?*

We can't kill openness to protect openness
How might we wrap the anguish into a project psyche and exploit it to unashamedly reveal a more fragile America which will yet sustain its primary advocacy for openness and freedom — an advocacy, rare in history, which paradoxically makes us vulnerable to those who hold a very different point of view. We look for the courage to sustain our constitutionally guaranteed openness that (may) facilitate its own destruction. And we Americans can't kill openness to protect openness. At the WTC, we will attempt to construct a (revised) normalcy that propels our unique vision of citizenship far into an otherwise indeterminate historic future.

Citizens

The WTC design solution should not zone the site based on conventional urban land parcel dividing lines and zoning subdivisions, e.g. commercial buildings over here (following the usual rules — floor plate and height/efficiency), and a memorial over there; or, commercial up here, memorial down there. And the project should not be segregated either vertically or horizontally into prosaic and esoteric, utilitarian and remembrance zones.

The design vision must be ecumenical and egalitarian. It needs to hear and re-echo the voices of America. The project must be conceptually legible and accessible, not one that makes a puzzle of its contents. This does not obviate the sublime and the esoteric, but it insists on their clarity. The form(s) are not yet invented to do this job. And form may not be the ultimate key. But the project won't belong to a recognized pedigree of buildings, monuments, landscapes, installations, sculptures, or high-rise office precedents, though it may include aspects of all those.

Music Music Music

If there is any art form that, inherent in its conception, can carry these conflicting sensibilities and simultaneously transform and resolve them, it is music. We should require sound and performance on the site. Contradictory needs are at the center of the WTC discussion. WTC proposals to this point have chosen one side or the other; normalcy or abnormalcy; horror or horror transcended; America endures or America revised. The music experience has the potential to transcend the (intellectually) irreconcilable. (As does architecture.)

A new American lyric

A 19th century Danish philosopher, Søren Kierkegaard, once referred to his written investigation of human affairs as a "dialectical lyric." Contradictory human tendencies were delineated intellectually, then transcended by the power of the art form itself. *By analogy, the solution for the new WTC project should intellectualize the contradictions intrinsic to the problem, then produce a transcendent conception of land form and landscape, buildings, music, and performance.*

The new WTC can reaffirm what is durable in America's advocacy and simultaneously reconfigure that advocacy: The WTC as dialectical lyric.

The proposed design team is prepared to team with the citizens of New York and America to develop this profound and complex conception. To borrow from TS Eliot, we will

"Not fare well,
But fare forward, voyagers."

Originally written for the World Trade Center Competition for the Lower Manhattan Development Corporation, September 16, 2002.

The Road is Better than the Inn

Thom Mayne

—

Several years ago, while SCI-Arc was packing to move downtown, I was rummaging in the old Beethoven Street library and came across a ragged, out of print book of quotations sitting on a shelf between Confucius' sayings and Mao's *Little Red Book*. The cover was tattered and the book itself appeared to be old, disheveled, and difficult to read.

The editor appeared to be a Thom M... The last name was virtually illegible. Nevertheless, given the extraordinary contents I discovered there, I've decided to share what remains of the text with you. I think you'll find some of it philosophically strident, some touchingly personal, and some strangely self-effacing.

Here's what I found:

> I will tell you what I will do and what I will not do. I will not serve that in which I no longer believe, whether it call itself modern, postmodern, new urban or blob, and I will try to express myself in architecture as freely as I can and as wholly as I can, using for my defense the only arms I allow myself to use — drawings, models, and cunning.
>
> **— Stephen Daedalus**
> **(apologies to James Joyce)**

> I will tell you what I do not fear. I do not fear to be alone or to be spurned by a client, or to leave whatever conceptual strategy I have for another. And I am not afraid to make a design mistake, even a great mistake.
>
> **— Stephen Daedalus**
> **(ditto)**

For architecture to possess greatness two things must come together: Greatness of spirit in those who accomplish it and greatness of spirit in those who experience it. No architecture possesses greatness in itself, though it involves the conception of entire cities, the construction of colossal infrastructure or the design of vast public buildings and squares. The breath of history has blown away many things of that kind as though they were flakes of snow.

It can also happen that an architect of supreme force conceives a project which strikes a reef and sinks from sight, having produced no impression; a brief, sharp echo, and all is over. History has virtually nothing to report about such truncated and neutralized events. And so whenever we see an architectural event approaching, we are overcome with the fear that those who experience it will force it onto the reef.

— **Nietzsche,** *Untimely Meditations*
(with apologies to Friedrich Nietzsche)

I do not know much about Gods; but I think that architecture is a strong God, sullen, untamed and intractable, patient to some degree; recognized as a frontier; untrustworthy as a conveyor of commerce; a problem confronting the builder. The problem once solved, the God is sometimes ignored by the dwellers in cities. Ever implacable, the architecture God sustains her seasons and rages, destroyer and reminder of what people choose to forget.

— **Eliot,** *The Dry Salvages*
(apologies to TS Eliot)

The audience the architect is looking to seduce is not a few specific and visible individuals. It's the great throng of invisible people! Listen, that's another chapter to be developed in architectural theory: The invisibility of the audience! That's what makes for the terrifying modernity of the architect's character. He's showing off, not for you or for me, but for the whole world. And what is the whole world? An infinity with no faces! An abstraction.

— **Kundera,** *Slowness*
(apologies to Milan Kundera)

Two and two make four is like a cocky NASDAQ salesman standing across your path with arms raised and a defiant air. I agree that two and two make four is an excellent thing; but to give everything its due, Thom M. knows that two and two makes five is also a very fine thing.

> — Dostoyevsky, *The Underground Man*
> (apologies to Fyodor Dostoyevsky)

Yet there is beauty in the thought that this architect who knows that he must die can wrest from the disdainful splendor of the nebulae an architectural music of the spheres, and broadcast it across the years to come, bestowing on it messages as yet unknown.

In that house of shadows where Gaudi still constructs his models, all the illustrious shapes, from the architects of the caverns onward, follow each movement of the trembling hand that is drafting for them a new lease on survival — or on sleep.

> — Malraux, *Voices of Silence*
> (apologies to André Malraux)

At the end of the text, I located a single intriguing drawing with a figure you may recognize as Don Quixote, and a caption that reads:

The road is better than the inn.

> — (apologies to Pablo Picasso)

Introduction to Thom Mayne lecture, SCI-Arc, November 13, 2002.

About the author

Eric Owen Moss holds masters degrees in Architecture from both Harvard University and the University of California at Berkeley.

Eric Owen Moss Architects was founded in 1973. The office, located in Los Angeles, California, is currently staffed with twenty-five professionals designing and constructing projects in the United States and around the world.

The firm has garnered over sixty design awards from *Progressive Architecture* magazine and the American Institute of Architects. In 1999, Moss won the Academy Award in Architecture from the American Academy of Arts and Letters. In 2001, the firm won the LAAIA Gold Medal for Design, and in 2003, Moss won the Gold Medal Distinguished Alumni Award from the University of California at Berkeley.

There are ten published monographs on the Moss office, including three by Rizzoli and one, *Gnostic Architecture*, by Monacelli Press. Most recent is *Eric Owen Moss — The Uncertainty of Doing*, published by Skira in 2006. *Eric Owen Moss — Provisional Paradigms* will be published by Marsilio in 2007.

Eric Owen Moss continues to build, teach, lecture and exhibit. In 2002, the firm won two competitions in St. Petersburg, Russia, one for the New

Mariinsky Theater, the second for the redevelopment of New Holland.

In 2003, Eric Owen Moss Architects won the international competition for the Queens Museum of Art in New York. In 2006, the Moss office won the City of the Future competition — LA, NY, Chicago — sponsored by the History Channel.

The Moss firm has been featured regularly at the Venice Biennale, with exhibits that have included, in 2002, the controversial proposal for the New Mariinsky Theater in St. Petersburg, at the Russian Pavilion, and, in 2004, the international competition entries for the National Library in Mexico City and the Smithsonian Institute. In 2006, the firm exhibited the Los Angeles/Culver City project in the Cities, Architecture, and Society section of the Biennale.

Eric Moss first taught at SCI-Arc in 1974, and was appointed director in 2002. He has held chairs at Yale and Harvard universities, and appointments at the University of Applied Arts in Vienna and the Royal Academy of Fine Arts in Copenhagen.

Eric Owen Moss received the 2007 Arnold Brunner Memorial Prize from the American Academy of Arts and Letters for "a significant contribution to architecture as an art."